ANDREW CARNEGIE

Other titles in *Historical American Biographies*

Alexander Graham Bell
Inventor and Teacher
ISBN 0-7660-1096-1

Andrew Carnegie
Steel King and
Friend to Libraries
ISBN 0-7660-1212-3

Annie Oakley
Legendary Sharpshooter
ISBN 0-7660-1012-0

Benjamin Franklin
Founding Father and Inventor
ISBN 0-89490-784-0

Buffalo Bill Cody
Western Legend
ISBN 0-7660-1015-5

Clara Barton
Civil War Nurse
ISBN 0-89490-778-6

Dolley Madison
Courageous First Lady
ISBN 0-7660-1092-9

Jane Addams
Nobel Prize Winner and
Founder of Hull House
ISBN 0-7660-1094-5

Jeb Stuart
Confederate Cavalry General
ISBN 0-7660-1013-9

Jefferson Davis
President of the Confederacy
ISBN 0-7660-1064-3

Jesse James
Legendary Outlaw
ISBN 0-7660-1055-4

John Wesley Powell
Explorer of the Grand Canyon
ISBN 0-89490-783-2

Lewis and Clark
Explorers of the Northwest
ISBN 0-7660-1016-3

Martha Washington
First Lady
ISBN 0-7660-1017-1

Paul Revere
Rider for the Revolution
ISBN 0-89490-779-4

Robert E. Lee
Southern Hero of the Civil War
ISBN 0-89490-782-4

Robert Fulton
Inventor and
Steamboat Builder
ISBN 0-7660-1141-0

Stonewall Jackson
Confederate General
ISBN 0-89490-781-6

Susan B. Anthony
Voice for Women's
Voting Rights
ISBN 0-89490-780-8

Thomas Alva Edison
Inventor
ISBN 0-7660-1014-7

Historical American Biographies

ANDREW CARNEGIE

Steel King and Friend to Libraries

Zachary Kent

Enslow Publishers, Inc.

40 Industrial Road   PO Box 38
Box 398   Aldershot
Berkeley Heights, NJ 07922 Hants GU12 6BP
USA   UK

http://www.enslow.com

Copyright © 1999 by Zachary Kent

Library of Congress Cataloging-in-Publication Data

Kent, Zachary.
    Andrew Carnegie : steel king and friend to libraries / Zachary Kent.
       p. cm.— (Historical American biographies)
    Includes bibliographical references (p.   ) and index.
    Summary: A biography of the Scottish immigrant who made a fortune
in the steel industry and used much of it for philanthropic causes.
    ISBN 0-7660-1212-3
    1. Carnegie, Andrew, 1835–1919. 2. United States—Biography—
Juvenile literature. 3. Philanthropists—United States—Biography—
Juvenile literature. 4. Industrialists—United States—Biography—Juvenile
literature. 5. Steel industry and trade—United States—History—
Juvenile literature. [1. Carnegie, Andrew, 1835–1919. 2. Industrialists.
3. Philanthropists.] I. Title. II. Series.
CT275.C3K46 1999
338.7'672'092
[B]—DC21   98-3160
                                                CIP
                                                AC

Printed in the United States of America

10 9 8 7 6 5 4 3

Illustration Credits: Enslow Publishers, Inc., pp. 37, 79, 98; Library of
Congress, pp. 8, 12, 14, 19, 26, 42, 48, 53, 56, 67, 71, 83, 88, 91, 97,
102, 109, 113; National Archives, pp. 46, 55, 59.

Cover Illustration: Library of Congress (Inset); © Corel Corporation
(Background—Molten Steel Being Poured).

CONTENTS

1

"THE RICHEST MAN IN THE WORLD"

In the year 1900, cargo ships carrying tons of iron ore from mines in Michigan, Wisconsin, and Minnesota steamed across the waters of the Great Lakes. Along the busy harbor docks of Conneaut, Ohio, giant shovel cranes scooped the iron ore from the ships and filled waiting railroad freight cars. Throughout each day, their whistles screaming, locomotives pulled loaded ore trains southward along the tracks to Pittsburgh, Pennsylvania, to the mills of the Carnegie Steel Company.

Inside the Carnegie mills, great blast furnaces reduced the iron ore to molten iron. From the blast furnaces, workers poured the molten iron into giant mixers and then into converters, changing the fiery liquid metal into steel. Huge ladles poured the red-hot fluid into molds made of cast iron. After the steel hardened, the molds were removed, and ingots of hardened steel remained. Next, great rollers squeezed the ingots into bars, sheets, and strips. In the Carnegie steelyards, foremen shouted commands as workers loaded the steel onto freight cars for shipment around the world.[1]

Carnegie steel had many uses. Across the United States, Mexico, Europe, China, and Japan, railroad workers laid miles of Carnegie steel rails. In American cities from New York to San Francisco,

On Lake Erie, steam shovels unload iron-ore barges and load freight cars bound for the Carnegie steel mills.

steelworkers riveted girders and beams in the construction of tall skyscrapers. In shipyards, thick plates of Carnegie steel were welded together to create armored navy ships. Factories fashioned Carnegie steel into pipe, rods, tubes, and wire. Bars and sheets of Carnegie steel were sold to manufacturers of tools, stoves, and hundreds of factory and household products.

The Carnegie Steel Company produced 2.97 million tons of steel in 1900. One man, sixty-five-year-old Andrew Carnegie, sat at the head of this industrial empire, the largest steel company in the world. When the year ended, bookkeepers reported that the company had made an annual profit of $40 million. Carnegie's personal share of this money was $25 million.

"Where is there such a business?" Carnegie joyfully exclaimed.[2]

Competition

For years, Andrew Carnegie had easily beaten all his competition. But in 1900, some companies that had been buying his iron and steel were being combined into large companies called trusts. To save the expense of buying Carnegie steel, the trusts intended to build their own steel mills. Leading this movement was millionaire banker J. P. Morgan, who had organized the National Tube Company. Carnegie saw that Morgan's trust posed a threat to his own business.

To meet the challenge, Carnegie telegraphed an urgent message to his partners: "Crisis has arrived, only one policy open; start at once hoop, rod, wire, nail mills. . . . Have no fear as to result, victory certain. Spend freely for finishing mills, railroads, boat lines."[3] Carnegie ordered a new tube factory built on the company's property at Conneaut. He drew up plans to build a new railroad across the state of Pennsylvania. Carnegie announced that he would soon manufacture more than just raw steel. He would make finished products, transport them to market himself, and expand his industrial empire. He would remain the world's leading steel producer no matter what it took, by whatever methods necessary.

Carnegie's business rivals rushed to J. P. Morgan for help. They knew they could not hope to compete. Carnegie had enough money and power to drive every steel company in the United States out of business. "If Carnegie begins to make tubes," exclaimed hundreds of frightened manufacturers, "he may decide later to make axes, ploughs, machinery. He may wipe us all out with this new policy."[4]

"GREAT STEEL WAR," shrieked banner newspaper headlines as the competition heightened for control of America's steel industry.[5] The calls on Morgan became more frequent, from both the railroad men and the steel men. Carnegie had to be stopped, and there seemed to be only one solution—buy him out.

J. P. Morgan Makes an Offer

In December 1900, Charles Schwab, the president of the Carnegie Steel Company, gave a speech in New York City. Eighty of the nation's top business leaders, investors, and bankers gathered at the exclusive University Club to hear Schwab speak on the future of America's steel industry. In his talk, Schwab insisted that a single, giant American steel company would be a total success. Among the guests that evening sat J. P. Morgan, listening with keen interest.

A few days afterward, Morgan invited Schwab to a private meeting. The two men sat talking in the great library of Morgan's home from nine o'clock at night until five o'clock the next morning. Schwab again described the great profits a single, super steel company could make. When dawn arrived, Morgan finally declared, "Well, if Andy wants to sell, I'll buy. Go and find his price."[6]

The Pierpont Morgan Library
Wealthy John Pierpont (J. P.) Morgan enjoyed collecting rare books, letters, drawings, and documents. By the early 1900s, his collection had grown so large that he built a private library in which to store it next to his mansion on East Thirty-sixth Street in New York City. Today the Pierpont Morgan Library is open to the public.

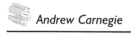

Millionaire banker J. P. Morgan (1837–1913). His famous bank on Wall Street in New York City became known as the House of Morgan.

Schwab went first to Carnegie's wife, Louise. He knew that Louise Carnegie wanted her aging husband to retire from business. She suggested that Schwab approach her husband on the golf course. Carnegie was always in his best mood immediately after a golf game, especially if he played well. The next morning at the St. Andrews Golf Club in Westchester County, New York, Schwab made sure Carnegie won their game. Later, in the clubhouse, Schwab revealed Morgan's offer. Carnegie sat silently a moment, and then said he would take the night to think it over.

When Schwab arrived at the Carnegie mansion the next day, Carnegie handed him a piece of paper. Written in pencil was the amount Carnegie demanded for his company: $480 million. Without delay, Schwab carried the paper to J. P. Morgan's office. The banker glanced only briefly at the paper before he calmly said, "I accept this price."[7] The great new company formed by Morgan and his business partners would be called the United States (U.S.) Steel Corporation.

No More Grasping for Dollars

When the contracts for the sale of Carnegie Steel were completed, J. P. Morgan visited Carnegie's Fifty-first Street home in New York City to shake hands on the deal. Upon leaving, Morgan stopped in the doorway and said, "Mr. Carnegie, I want to congratulate you on being the richest man in the world."[8]

It was true that Andrew Carnegie had become rich. As the majority partner in the Carnegie Steel Company, his share of the sale amounted to about $300 million, a stunning fortune. Next, Carnegie surprised the world with his sense of charity. Carnegie had fulfilled the American dream, rising from poverty to become incredibly rich. Now he had the time and the money to take up his real interest, the business of giving.

The First Billion-Dollar Company
In February 1901, Carnegie Steel and seven other companies merged to become the U.S. Steel Corporation, the first company in the world valued at more than $1 billion. Elbert H. Gary was elected U.S. Steel's first chief executive officer. The steel-mill city of Gary, Indiana, is named after him.

THE MACMILLION.

[Mr. CARNEGIE, the Scottish-American millionaire, has provided £2,000,000 for the establishment of free education at four of the Scottish Universities —Edinburgh, Glasgow, St. Andrew's, Aberdeen.]

This cartoon, showing Andrew Carnegie scattering his riches, appeared in Punch *magazine in 1901 after Carnegie donated $10 million to four Scottish universities.*

"Among the saddest of all spectacles to me," Carnegie had once declared, "is that of an elderly man occupying his last years grasping for more dollars."[9] For years he had stated that wealthy Americans had an obligation to do things for the benefit of others. Now he intended to show what he meant. During the next eighteen years, he would give away the bulk of his fortune to worthy causes. In the end, his gifts would amount to over $350 million—an overwhelming sum to be donated by one individual. The value of that sum today would equal about $4.5 billion.[10]

Carnegie's gifts included more than twenty-eight hundred library buildings to various towns and cities. He donated organs to churches and built concert halls, an art gallery, a museum, and a technical school. He made gifts to four hundred colleges and universities. He used his money to finance scientific expeditions and research laboratories. He established a fund to reward acts of heroism, and he provided pensions for the needy.

Carnegie's life had begun with hardship, but he ended his days at the height of success. Step by step, with hard work and cheerful energy, he built up a giant steel industry. Then deliberately and systematically he gave away his wealth for the betterment of all. The poor immigrant boy from Scotland had grown into the greatest philanthropist of his time.

2

THE
SCOTTISH
WEAVER'S SON

"To begin, then, I was born in Dunfermline," Carnegie would recall, "in the attic of [a] small one-story house, corner of Moodie Street and Priory Lane, on the 25th of November, 1835."[1] He was the first child of William and Margaret Morrison Carnegie. His father was a weaver of damask, a sturdy linen cloth. In Dunfermline, Scotland, many skilled people worked in the weaving trade.

When Andrew was still a baby, the Carnegies moved from Moodie Street to a house on Edgar Street. The living space upstairs was more comfortable for the growing family, and there was enough room downstairs for four looms. While young apprentices kept busy at three of the looms, William Carnegie worked at the fourth.

Little Andrew would watch in awe as his father worked at the loom. His father's feet pumped the treadles while his arms and hands went back and forth, working the driver stick and the batten, pulling the damask thread horizontally through the woof. With complex and rapid movement, the weaver created patterned cloth, the material slowly rolling out before the child's eyes. Andrew would stare in wonder at the result of his father's craftsmanship. As his father worked, designs emerged on the cloth, containing leaves, birds, flowers, and fruit.

When Andrew was four, in January 1840, William and Margaret Carnegie had a second child, a daughter named Ann. Sadly, the delicate baby died while still an infant. Three years later, though, in 1843, the crying of another new baby could be heard in the Carnegie house. Andrew happily carried news of his baby brother, Tom, through the streets to neighbors and friends.

That same year, eight-year-old Andrew began attending school. "My parents had promised," he later recalled, "that I should never be sent to school until I asked leave to go."[2] When Andrew showed no interest in going to school, his parents asked the local schoolmaster, Robert Martin, what they should do. Martin had an idea. He invited Andrew to join

children his age on a school trip. Andrew's parents were greatly relieved when, soon afterward, their son asked them for permission to attend Martin's school.

Learning Lessons

At Martin's school, as many as 180 children crowded into a single large room. To keep the attention of so many students, Martin sometimes slapped those who misbehaved with a small leather strap. "Ye hae na [you have not] been put into this world to enjoy yoursel', but to do yair duty," the schoolteacher often reminded his pupils in his Scottish accent. Andrew did his duty and studied hard. His schoolmates teased him by calling him "Martin's pet."[3]

Each day before school, Andrew hurriedly ate his breakfast of oatmeal porridge. Then, he ran to the public well at the head of Moodie Street. It was Andrew's job each morning to fetch a bucket of water. Few houses in the 1840s had plumbing, and Andrew's mother needed the water for cooking and washing. "In the performance of these duties I was often late for school," Andrew remembered, "but the master, knowing the cause, forgave the lapses."[4]

As a hobby, Andrew enjoyed keeping pigeons and rabbits. His father hammered together a hutch for these pets in the backyard. On Saturdays, Andrew persuaded his friends to help him gather food for the rabbits. "My young playmates . . . were content to gather dandelions and clover for a whole season with me," he recalled.[5] The reason for

Andrew Carnegie at the age of nine. The boy who was "Martin's pet" at school would have a lifelong interest in reading and books.

their helpfulness was Andrew's promise to name newborn rabbits after each of them.

Andrew's best friend was his cousin, George "Dod" Lauder. The two boys spent many afternoons and evenings in the High Street grocery store run by Andrew's uncle, George Lauder. When business was slow, Lauder would talk history by the hour. Many of the kings, queens, and princes of early Scotland were born, lived, or were buried in Dunfermline, once Scotland's capital. From his uncle, Andrew learned about such Scottish heroes as William Wallace and Robert Bruce and about the Scottish poetry of Robert Burns. The boy also learned about the United States and its heroes—George Washington, Thomas Jefferson, Benjamin Franklin.[6]

Uncle Lauder loved music, especially traditional Scottish music played on the violin, and he could sing all the old Scottish ballads. He also loved nature and knew the names of wildflowers and

The Story of William Wallace
Actor Mel Gibson directed and starred in a movie about the life of medieval Scottish patriot William Wallace, who led a famous revolt against King Edward I of England in 1296. His rebels were eventually defeated, and Wallace was executed for treason. Gibson's movie about Wallace, entitled *Braveheart*, won the Academy Award for Best Picture in 1995.

birds. He often took Dod and Andrew hiking in the countryside, where they explored the local ruins and relics of Scotland's history.

Chartist Politics in Scotland

Andrew's father was a regular speaker at Chartist political rallies in Dunfermline in the 1840s. Andrew's uncle Tom Morrison was a well-known Chartist, too. The Chartists complained that Queen Victoria and the royal members of Great Britain's House of Lords had too much control over the government. Chartists called for a more democratic government for Scotland and for greater voting rights for the working class. They proposed a People's Charter that demanded the secret ballot and annual national elections. Andrew remembered hearing his father address one large outdoor meeting:

I had wedged my way in under the legs of the hearers, and at one cheer louder than all the rest I could not restrain my enthusiasm. Looking up to the man under whose legs I had found protection I informed him that was my father speaking. He lifted me on his shoulder and kept me there.[7]

One of the wealthiest families in Dunfermline owned Pittencrieff, a large estate. Behind the great stone walls of Pittencrieff lay the most beautiful park in all the region. It was at Pittencrieff that the historic ruins of a monastery and castle stood. Each May, the owners of Pittencrieff opened the park to the public. But they refused to allow the Carnegie and the Morrison families to enter because of their radical politics. Often Andrew stood at the gate, wishing for the chance to go inside.

The Power of the Steam Engine

In 1843, a steam-powered textile mill opened in Dunfermline. An industrial revolution was sweeping across Great Britain. Factory owners could hire unskilled women and children to attend the new power-driven looms and make cloth cheaply. Hand-loom weavers like Andrew's father were faced with sudden disaster. Before the end of the year, William Carnegie was forced to dismiss one of his apprentices and to sell one of his four looms. The second and third looms soon followed. As his business shrank and hand-loom work disappeared, the Carnegies had to move from Edgar Street back to a smaller cottage on Moodie Street.[8]

Margaret Carnegie added to the family's dwindling income by opening a small store in the front room of the house. She went out early each morning to find the cheapest and freshest vegetables to sell in her little shop. She sold flour, salt, cabbages, potatoes, tobacco, and candy to the people of the neighborhood. At night she stayed up late, working as a cobbler, stitching shoes. "We were not . . . reduced to anything like poverty compared with many of our neighbors," Andrew gratefully recalled. "I do not know to what lengths of [sacrifice] my mother would not have gone that she might see her two boys wearing large white collars, and trimly dressed."[9]

In the summer of 1847, another large steam-powered textile mill opened in Dunfermline. Four hundred weavers found employment there, but the mill threw hundreds of others out of work. Gray smoke poured out of the busy factory's chimneys and floated over the town. But shutters covered the windows of idle hand-loom shops. One winter evening Andrew's father returned home after searching for weaving orders and quietly announced to his son, "Andra, I can get nae mair [no more] work."[10]

The Land of Opportunity

The Carnegies had relatives in America. Two of Mrs. Carnegie's sisters, Annie Aitken and Kitty Hogan, had journeyed with their husbands to Pittsburgh, Pennsylvania, in 1840 to start new lives. In letters,

Mrs. Carnegie's sisters had often urged her to join them. One sister wrote,

> This country is far better for the workingman than the old one, and there is room enough to spare, notwithstanding the thousands that flock into her borders every year. As for myself, I like it much better than at home, for in fact you seem to breathe a freer atmosphere here.[11]

After long discussions, Andrew's parents decided that the family should leave Scotland.

"The decision was taken to sell the looms and furniture by auction," Andrew remembered. "And my father's sweet voice sang often to mother, brother, and me:

> *To the West, to the West, to the land of the free,*
> *where the mighty Missouri rolls down to the sea;*
> *Where a man is a man even though he must toil*
> *And the poorest may gather the fruits of the soil.*[12]

Margaret Carnegie burned with shame at having to leave Scotland in defeat and poverty. She was determined, however, to see that her sons had a chance for a better future than Dunfermline offered. In early spring of 1848 the Carnegies sold their furniture. The family borrowed money from Mrs. Ailie Henderson to pay for ship passage, and in May, the Carnegies finally set off by stagecoach from Dunfermline on the first part of their great journey. They traveled to the city of Edinburgh, and Uncle Lauder came along to say good-bye. It was a tearful parting.

"We were rowed over in a small boat to the Edinburgh steamer in the Firth [Bay] of Forth," Andrew remembered. "As I was about to be taken from the small boat to the steamer, I rushed to Uncle Lauder and clung round his neck, crying out: 'I cannot leave you! I cannot leave you!' I was torn from him by a kind sailor who lifted me up on the deck of the steamer."[13]

From Edinburgh, the Carnegies made their way by canal to the city of Glasgow. They were herded aboard the ship *Wiscasset* and assigned their bunks. On the morning of May 17, 1848, the *Wiscasset* moved out into the Atlantic on the outgoing tide.[14] At the age of twelve, Andrew was on his way to the United States, the land of opportunity.

3

RISE OF AN IMMIGRANT BOY

The ship *Wiscasset* plowed forward through great green ocean waves during its seven-week voyage across the Atlantic. On the fiftieth day of its journey, the ship dropped anchor at Castle Garden in New York Harbor. Three more weeks of hard travel carried the Carnegie family from New York City westward by riverboat and canal boat. At last, they reached Pittsburgh, Pennsylvania.

Pittsburgh stands on a point of land where the Monongahela and Allegheny rivers meet to form the Ohio River. Easy river transportation had spurred Pittsburgh's growth as a center of industry. The Carnegies walked through muddy streets jammed with wagons, dray carts, and carriages. They

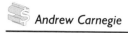

A ship of immigrants docks at Castle Garden in New York City. In 1848, 188,233 immigrants arrived in the United States from the countries that made up the kingdom of Great Britain: England, Ireland, Wales, and Scotland.

breathed city air thick with the smoke of factory chimneys.

Getting Settled

Mrs. Carnegie's two sisters, Kitty Hogan and Annie Aitken, had settled with their husbands on Rebecca Street in Barefoot Square, Slabtown, in Allegheny City. Allegheny lay across the river from Pittsburgh and is today a part of Pittsburgh. The Carnegies moved into two rooms on the second story of a house owned by the brother of Uncle Andrew Hogan. An abandoned loom stood in the downstairs shop. Andrew's father rented it from Andrew Hogan and began weaving damask tablecloths, which he peddled door-to-door.[1]

Andrew's mother found work sewing shoes for a neighborhood shoemaker named Henry Phipps. She tirelessly sat up late at night, stitching shoe leather for four dollars a week. Young Tom Carnegie was sent to school, but Andrew, with just five years of schooling, would get no more. Instead, he hoped to find a job, in order to help support the family.

Uncle Hogan's brother kindly suggested that Andrew might become a peddler, selling fruit and candy around the city docks. "My mother was sitting sewing at the moment," Andrew recalled, "but she sprang to her feet with outstretched hands and shook them in his face. 'What! my son a peddler and go among rough men upon the wharves! I would rather throw him into the Allegheny River.'"[2] She wanted Andrew to amount to something better in life, to become useful, honored, and respected.

Andrew's father had little success selling his handmade tablecloths. After a few weeks, he had to take work in a nearby Allegheny textile mill. Thirteen-year-old Andrew also went with him and found employment. Father and son arose every morning at six o'clock and walked to the mill. There, William Carnegie tended a large power-driven loom,

while Andrew worked as a bobbin boy. Bobbins were the large wooden spools on which thread was wound. The power looms unwound the thread as they made fabric, and it was Andrew's duty to replace the bobbins and keep the looms supplied with thread. Father and son worked in the hot, dusty, noisy factory until six o'clock each evening. For six days' work, Andrew earned $1.20. "It was a hard life," he later remembered. Andrew's father found factory work so depressing that after a few months he returned to his hand-loom to make his own tablecloths. But Andrew stayed on. "The hours hung heavily upon me," he would recall, "and in the work itself I took no pleasure."[3]

Before long, a manufacturer of wooden bobbins in Allegheny named John Hay offered Andrew a job in his factory. For two dollars a week, Andrew accepted the offer. In Hay's factory, Andrew was stationed alone in the cellar, running a small steam engine by feeding coal into the boiler. He had to supply enough steam power for all the machinery upstairs. But he constantly feared that if he fired the boiler too high, it would explode. The great responsibility made him very anxious.

He had another disagreeable duty as well. After the bobbins were made, they were brought down to the cellar. Andrew had to dip them in large vats of oil to preserve the wood. In the cramped, rough basement, the steam engine noisily thumped and whined, and Andrew breathed the nauseous stench of oil. He was a lonely and frightened boy, but still he recalled, "My hopes were high, and I looked every day for some change to take place."[4]

Luckily, one day John Hay found he needed a clerk. He asked Andrew to show him a sample of his penmanship. The boy's bold, open handwriting pleased Hay, and he invited Andrew to come up from the cellar from time to time to write business letters and bills. At night, Andrew took a course in bookkeeping to make himself more valuable as a clerk. He went to class in the winter, trudging across the bridge to Pittsburgh and back after a twelve-hour day amid bobbins and boilers, all at the age of fourteen.[5]

The Telegraph Office

Andrew's Uncle Hogan often played checkers to relax after work. Among his fellow players was David Brooks, who managed a telegraph office in Pittsburgh. Inventor Samuel F. B. Morse had first harnessed the energy of electricity in 1836. Morse's telegraph was a machine that sent electric impulses for miles through a wire. Using Morse's code of short dots and long dashes to represent the letters of the alphabet, messages could travel great distances. By 1850, telegraph companies were stringing wire and opening offices all over the United States.[6]

One evening while playing checkers, Andrew's Uncle Hogan learned some interesting news.

"When I returned home from work," Andrew later remembered, "I was told that Mr. David Brooks . . . had asked my Uncle Hogan if he knew where a good boy could be found to act as messenger."[7] Brooks would pay $2.50 per week.

Andrew jumped at the chance to escape the bobbin-factory cellar and the oil vat. The next morning, dressed in a white shirt and his one good suit, Andrew, accompanied by his father, walked the two miles to the O'Reilly telegraph office at the corner of Third and Wood streets in downtown Pittsburgh. Outside the building, Andrew asked his father to wait. He preferred to go inside alone. He admitted later that he was afraid his father's broad Scottish accent might be embarrassing.[8]

In another few moments, Andrew stood before Brooks. The boy was small for his fourteen years, but his eager manner convinced Brooks to give the boy a chance. Brooks asked when he could start work, and Andrew quickly answered that he was ready to begin immediately. "Having got myself in I proposed to stay there if I could," Andrew later declared. He instantly began to learn his new duties. It was some time before he remembered that his father was still waiting outside. He ran down to the street corner and told him that he had the job. He had become a telegraph messenger boy. "From the dark cellar running a steam-engine at two dollars a week, begrimed with coal dirt," he later declared, "I was lifted into paradise, yes, heaven, as it seemed to me. . . . I felt that my foot was upon the ladder and that I was bound to climb."[9]

Bright and observant, young Andrew Carnegie soon knew as much about Pittsburgh's business affairs as anyone in town. The telegraph messages he carried took him into offices, banks, newspapers, and private homes. Pittsburgh in 1850 was a city of forty-five thousand people. In order to learn Pittsburgh business addresses, Carnegie developed a plan:

> I . . . began to note the signs of these houses up one side of the street and down the other. At nights I exercised my memory by naming in succession the various firms. Before long I could shut my eyes and, beginning at the foot of a business street, call off the names of the firms in proper order.[10]

With his fine memory, he could soon deliver his messages swiftly to any address in town.

Business rapidly increased at the telegraph office. As other messenger boys were hired, Carnegie loyally brought in friends from his Allegheny neighborhood: Robert Pitcairn, David McCargo, Henry Oliver. The boys became easily recognized around Pittsburgh, dressed in their dark green uniform jackets and short trousers.

The Messenger Boy

"A messenger boy in those days," Carnegie recalled, "had many pleasures. There were wholesale fruit stores, where a pocketful of apples was sometimes

to be had for the prompt delivery of a message [and bakeries] where sweet cakes were sometimes given to him."[11] Carnegie also enjoyed free admission to the town's theaters to watch the plays performed.

The messengers were allowed an extra charge of ten cents for messages delivered far beyond the business district. Carnegie suggested that the boys put these extra charges together. As treasurer of the "dime message" fund, Andrew divided the money equally at the end of each week.[12]

By the summer of 1850, fourteen-year-old Andrew Carnegie was bringing home more than $2.50 a week. He gladly added his earnings to the money his mother earned sewing shoes and to the little bit his father brought home from selling table-cloths. "Day by day," Carnegie explained, "as mother could spare a silver half-dollar, it was carefully placed in a stocking and hid until two hundred were gathered."[13] It was a happy day when Margaret Carnegie sent that sum to Scotland to repay the money loaned for the family's passage to America. Not long afterward, the Hogans moved to Ohio. The Carnegies rented the Hogans' small house down by the river. Andrew and his brother, Tom, shouted joyfully at the idea of a house of their own.

Andrew Carnegie also found a chance to improve his education. Rich old Colonel James Anderson had a personal library of four hundred books. Since there was no public library in

Allegheny, Anderson generously opened his home to young working boys each Saturday and allowed them to borrow a book from week to week. Carnegie became his most faithful borrower. He later wrote, "Colonel Anderson opened to me the intellectual wealth of the world."[14] Among the books Carnegie read were *Bancroft's History of the United States* and the plays of William Shakespeare.

Telegraph Operator

Carnegie came early and swept out the telegraph office in the morning before it opened. It was then, he explained, that "the boys had an opportunity of practicing upon the telegraph instruments before the operators arrived." With practice, Carnegie soon could send messages to other telegraph boys in distant towns and receive their answers.

One morning, an unexpected urgent message came through from Philadelphia. Carnegie was the only one in the office able to take the message. He took the message and hurried to deliver it, and instead of being scolded, he was praised. He recalled, "It was not long before I was called sometimes to watch the instrument, while the operator wished to be absent, and in this way I learned the art of telegraphy."[15]

In those days the dots and dashes of incoming telegraph messages first became impressed upon a slip of paper. The operator read the markings to a copyist who would then translate them into writing. "But rumors had reached us," Carnegie remembered,

"that a man in the West had learned to . . . take a message by ear. This led me to practice the new method."[16] Quickly Carnegie trained himself to recognize the Morse code letters directly by their sounds, which saved much time.

Before long, sixteen-year-old Carnegie found himself promoted to telegraph operator. "I liked the boy's looks," recalled James D. Reid, superintendent of the telegraph line, "and it was very easy to see that though he was little he was full of spirit."[17] In a year and a half, Carnegie had risen from messenger boy to telegraph operator with a handsome salary of twenty-five dollars per month. He earned an additional dollar a day by making copies of the foreign news that came over the telegraph wires to be sold to the local newspapers. This enabled the Carnegies to buy a house of their own. Andrew had become the main support of the family.

Carnegie was reputed to be only the third operator in America who had learned to take

The Webster Literary Society
As a teenager, Andrew Carnegie formed the "Webster Literary Society," a small debating club. The members met in a room over Mr. Phipps's cobbler shop to discuss national politics, government, and philosophy.

messages by sound. It was such a rare skill that people sometimes came to the telegraph office just to watch him work. Pittsburgh businessmen chose Carnegie, clearly the city's most skilled telegrapher, to send their important messages. Thomas A. Scott, the newly appointed superintendent of the Western Division of the Pennsylvania Railroad, was especially impressed with him. Scott's work made him a constant caller at the telegraph office, and he relied on young Andrew Carnegie to send all his railroad messages.

Scott was amused by the boy's bustling efficiency and cheerfulness, his cleverness and energy. Soon Scott wondered if he might hire such a bright young man. While talking with one of Scott's clerks one day, Carnegie was surprised to hear of Scott's interest. Carnegie told the clerk that Scott could have him if he wanted him.

He grabbed at this new chance to advance himself. He guessed the growing railroad industry had even more potential than the telegraph. In February 1853, seventeen-year-old Andrew Carnegie left the telegraph office and went to work for Thomas Scott at the Pennsylvania Railroad.

4

YOUNG
RAILROAD
MAN

I have some news to tell you," Carnegie wrote to his uncle George Lauder. "I left my old place in the telegraph office and am now in the employ of the Pennsylvania Railroad Co."[1] In February 1853, he entered his new occupation as telegrapher, secretary, and general assistant to Thomas Scott. Scott liked the young man right away. Carnegie stood five feet three inches tall. He had a round, ruddy, boyish face, and his hair was of such a light and sandy color it appeared white. He always seemed to be full of enthusiasm and good-natured charm.

Like the telegraph, the railroad was a new invention, and the Pennsylvania Railroad was one of the fastest-growing railroad companies. By 1853, its single-track line stretched across Pennsylvania from Philadelphia to Pittsburgh. As Superintendent Scott's assistant, Carnegie often traveled along the railroad line to investigate maintenance problems, construction projects, and accidents. He talked with railroad customers and organized freight shipments. Most important, he sent the telegraph messages that helped the trains move swiftly and safely. By 1855, when Carnegie was twenty years old, Scott was giving him more and more responsibility.

One morning Carnegie arrived at the office and learned there had been a serious railroad accident. None of the freight trains could move in either direction, and no one could find Scott.[2] "Finally I

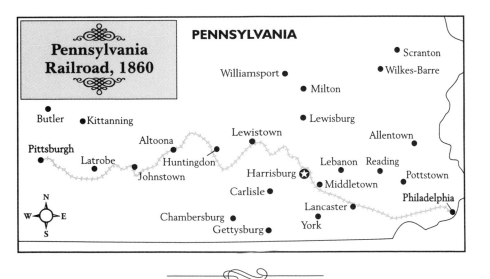

This map shows the route of the Pennsylvania Railroad, from Philadelphia to Pittsburgh, where Andrew Carnegie started working in 1853.

could not resist the temptation to plunge in, take the responsibility, give 'train orders,' and set matters going. . . ." Carnegie later explained.[3] He gave the orders in Scott's name, realizing that he risked dismissal, disgrace, perhaps even prison, if he made a mistake. When Scott at last reached the office, Carnegie explained what he had done and gave his boss the position of every train on the line. Expertly, but without permission, Carnegie had gotten the trains running smoothly again.

Scott said nothing at the time, and Carnegie felt very anxious until he heard from Mr. Franciscus, the freight department manager. Scott had told Franciscus, "Do you know what that little white-haired Scotch devil of mine did today? [He ran] every train on the division in my name, without the slightest authority."

"And did he do it all right?" Franciscus had asked.

"Oh, yes, all right!" Scott admitted with amusement in his voice.[4]

Carnegie's bold action and sense of responsibility raised his worth in Scott's opinion. When J. Edgar Thomson, the president of the railroad visited the Pittsburgh office, he greeted Carnegie with a smile and called him "Scott's Andy."[5]

In May 1856, Scott offered Carnegie a new opportunity, a chance to buy ten shares of valuable Adams Express Company stock. He even loaned

Carnegie the $610 needed for the purchase. "This was my first investment," Carnegie proudly recalled. He never forgot receiving his first Adams Express dividend of ten dollars. "I shall remember that check as long as I live. . . . It gave me the first penny of revenue from capital—something that I had not worked for with the sweat of my brow."[6]

In the autumn of 1856, Scott was promoted to general superintendent of the railroad. That meant a transfer to the central line offices in Altoona, Pennsylvania, eighty-five miles east of Pittsburgh. Twenty-one-year-old Carnegie went with him as a secretary, with a salary of fifty dollars a month. Carnegie brought along his mother and brother. He was the only wage earner in the Carnegie family now. Sadly, in October 1855, his father had died at the age of fifty-one, after a long illness. "Alas," wrote

Carnegie Loses a Payroll
Carnegie loved riding on railroad locomotives with the engineer. Once when traveling with a package of payroll money tucked under his vest, the rough ride shook the package loose. When Carnegie discovered that the package was gone, he begged the engineer to back up the train. Luckily, the valuable package was found lying beside the tracks.

Carnegie, "he passed away just as we were becoming able to give him leisure and comfort."[7]

Seizing on Luck

One day in 1858, while traveling by train on railroad business, Carnegie was approached by one of his fellow travelers. The stranger, Theodore Woodruff, told Carnegie that he had invented something new and important. Woodruff carried with him a small model of a sleeping car. Its unique design allowed railroad travelers to lie down and sleep during long train journeys. A regular passenger car during the day, it could be converted to a sleeping car at night by laying boards across the facing seats to form beds. Compartments above the seats could be opened and lowered by chains to provide additional beds. When curtains were drawn, passengers could sleep in comfort and privacy.

"I could not get that sleeping-car idea out of my mind," Carnegie declared after his lucky meeting.[8] He presented Woodruff's idea to President Thomson and Mr. Scott. The Pennsylvania Railroad quickly decided to develop the Woodruff sleeping cars. For his help in organizing the Woodruff Sleeping Car Company, Carnegie was given a one-eighth interest, costing him $217.50. Within a year, the Woodruff sleeping cars had become a stunning success, and Carnegie's investment in sleeping cars was soon paying him a profit of more than five thousand dollars a year.[9]

Division Superintendent Carnegie

In December 1859, Thomas A. Scott was promoted to vice president of the Pennsylvania Railroad Company, and Carnegie was rewarded for his own good work. He was named superintendent of the Western Division of the railroad with a salary of fifteen hundred dollars a year. Carnegie's sixteen-year-old brother, Tom, had learned telegraphy while living in Altoona. Carnegie hired Tom to be his secretary.

As division superintendent, Carnegie was responsible for the expanding Pennsylvania Railroad line from Pittsburgh westward through Ohio into Indiana. Carnegie bought a two-story house in suburban Homewood, fifteen miles northeast of Pittsburgh, and moved there with his mother. Spruce trees and flowerbeds filled the grassy yard. The social center of Homewood was Judge William Wilkins's home. Leila Addison, the judge's granddaughter, befriended Carnegie and helped him improve his grammar and taught him good manners. Carnegie's quick wit and good humor made him a lively companion. He gladly joined his Homewood friends at ice-skating parties, play-reading sessions, and weekly choir practices.[10]

During his first winter as division superintendent, Carnegie often worked without rest in the ice and snow. Cold weather, with frequent thawing and freezing, caused breaks in the cast-iron rails along

Andrew Carnegie sat for this photograph at the age of twenty-five,
when he was division superintendent of the Pennsylvania Railroad.

the railroad line. "At one time for eight days," Carnegie remembered, "I was constantly upon the line, day and night, at one wreck or obstruction after another."[11] Carnegie relentlessly pushed his work crews to repair damaged track and keep the trains running on schedule.

When the railroad company constructed its own telegraph line, Carnegie appointed his old friend and fellow messenger boy, David McCargo, superintendent of the telegraph department on March 11, 1859. Carnegie and McCargo became the first to employ young women as telegraph operators in the United States. "Our experience," Carnegie explained, "was that young women operators were more to be relied upon than young men."[12]

The Yankee Patriot

For more than thirty years, the moral issue of slavery had threatened to split the United States in two. In the rapidly industrializing North, thousands of European immigrants provided a cheap labor force. Most Northerners had no use for slavery, and many believed it to be cruel and immoral. In the South, however, owners of cotton, rice, and tobacco plantations depended on slave labor. The problem reached a crisis in the fall of 1860 when Abraham Lincoln of Illinois was elected the sixteenth president of the United States. Many Southerners feared Lincoln would abolish slavery. They insisted that the federal government had no right to force laws upon

Carnegie and the Prince of Wales
When Great Britain's young Prince of Wales, the future King Edward VII, visited America in 1860, scores of railroad men assisted him along his line of travel. But Andrew Carnegie was the only one who sprang forward and offered the prince an exciting ride on a locomotive.

the separate states. During the next few months, South Carolina, Florida, Georgia, Alabama, Texas, Mississippi, and Louisiana declared their independence and called themselves the Confederate States of America. In April 1861, Confederate militiamen attacked and captured Union Fort Sumter in the harbor of Charleston, South Carolina. Soon Virginia, North Carolina, Arkansas, and Tennessee also joined the Confederacy. The Civil War had begun.

Ten days after Fort Sumter surrendered, the United States War Department called Thomas Scott to Washington, D.C., to organize the North's railroad and telegraph lines. Washington seemed in danger of invasion at any moment. Confederate Virginians gathered to the south, and Confederate sympathizers in Maryland to the north had destroyed key railroad and telegraph lines, cutting off transportation and communication to the capital. President Lincoln waited anxiously for Northern troops to protect the capital. In this emergency, Scott telegraphed Carnegie for help. Carnegie, who was a loyal Union man, swiftly collected train men, trackmen, bridge builders, and other skilled workers and hurried toward Washington.

In Annapolis, Maryland, Carnegie's railroad workers, aided by volunteer troops, repaired the line into Annapolis Junction. In the early morning hours of April 25, 1861, a hastily improvised train was ready for its first run into Washington. Massachusetts and New York volunteer soldiers rode in the cars. Carnegie rode on the locomotive with the engineer and fireman. Near the outskirts of Washington, he noticed that the telegraph wires that ran beside the tracks had been yanked to the ground and pinned down with stakes. Stopping the train, Carnegie jumped down to remove the stakes. The wires, suddenly released, struck him full in the face, cutting a gash across his cheek and forehead. With blood streaming down his face, Carnegie rode the train into Washington, bringing the first troops to the defense of the capital.

In Washington, Carnegie's first task was to extend the Baltimore and Ohio Railroad track from the city depot down to the Potomac River. Long Bridge, over the Potomac, had to be rebuilt to assist in the movement of troops and heavy supply trains into Virginia. "Under the direction of Carnegie . . . the railroad [bridge] between Washington and

Alexandria was completed in the remarkable short period of seven days," recalled one of his telegraphers. "All hands, from Carnegie down, worked day and night to accomplish the task. . . ."[13] Carnegie established his headquarters in Alexandria, Virginia. Along the Orange & Alexandria Railroad southward, Carnegie's crew repaired the line and established telegraph stations at Alexandria, Burke Station, and Fairfax.

Union soldiers guard the Long Bridge. This bridge across the Potomac River, which Carnegie helped rebuild, was a vital military link between Washington, D.C., and Virginia.

Manassas Junction, Virginia, some thirty miles southwest of Washington, was an important railroad junction held by Confederate forces. In late July 1861, the first major battle of the Civil War was fought there beside a creek called Bull Run. During the battle, Carnegie supervised the Burke Station telegraph only a few miles away. Through the morning, Carnegie sent dispatches to Washington. The messages he received from the battlefield reported that the fight at Bull Run was a smashing victory for the North. But Confederate reinforcements in the afternoon changed the battle's outcome. Panicky Union troops could be seen rushing up the road from Bull Run. Carnegie's operator at Fairfax sent one final dispatch to Washington, "Our army is retreating." Carnegie kept the trains running back to Alexandria, filled with wounded soldiers, as long as he could.[14] "I went out there and loaded up train after train. . . ." Carnegie later exclaimed. "The rebels were reported to be close upon us and we were finally compelled to close Burke Station, the operator and myself leaving on the last train for Alexandria."[15] He narrowly escaped capture.

Back at the War Department in Washington, Carnegie assisted in organizing the fifteen-hundred-man United States Military Telegraph Corps, designed to maintain Union military communications during the war. Often, Carnegie saw President Lincoln at the War Department telegraph office,

This is a view of Burke Station, Virginia. During the Battle of Bull Run, Carnegie supervised the operation of the telegraph line here, until forced to retreat.

waiting for the latest military news. Carnegie later said of Lincoln, "His manners were perfect because [they were] natural; and he had a kind word for everybody, even the youngest boy in the office."[16]

Return to Pittsburgh

In the hot summer of 1861, while supervising the repair of a Virginia railroad bridge, Carnegie suffered a mild sunstroke. Exhausted from his work and suffering from the heat, Carnegie left Washington, D.C., in September and returned to his railroad work in Pittsburgh. He worked through the winter and became so weak and tired that in 1862, the Pennsylvania Railroad granted him three months' leave to rest. It was his first vacation in fourteen years.

In an effort to regain his health, he decided to take a trip to Scotland with his mother and a boyhood friend, Thomas Miller. They sailed on the *Aetna* on June 28, 1862, to Liverpool, England. Then, they traveled by train to Edinburgh, Scotland, and on to Dunfermline. In Dunfermline, he joyfully hugged Uncle Lauder and Cousin Dod and exchanged news with other relatives and friends. The strain and excitement of the trip, however, soon proved too much for him. A cold developed into pneumonia, and for six weeks he lay in bed, deathly ill with a fever. Only after his illness were he and his mother able to return to America.

The Foundation of a Fortune

During 1863 and 1864, Superintendent Carnegie proved himself daring and valuable to the Pennsylvania Railroad. He cleared railroad wrecks by burning the cars that blocked the line or by laying new tracks around them. He kept telegraph lines open twenty-four hours a day to help keep trains moving. He advised the construction of double tracks to enable trains to run both east and west at the same time and avoid delays.[17]

Carnegie made many personal investments during these war years, too. With the big profits from

his share in the Woodruff Sleeping Car Company, Carnegie bought shares in other enterprises. He invested in the Western Union Telegraph Company, the Iron City Forge, the Columbia Oil Company, and the Third National Bank of Pittsburgh. He invested in a construction company and in a Pittsburgh streetcar company. Carnegie founded the Freedom Iron Company for the purpose of manufacturing iron rails and the Pittsburgh Locomotive Works to make engines. By his twenty-ninth birthday, in 1864, he owned shares in more than a dozen different companies. In addition to his railroad salary of twenty-four hundred dollars a year, he was earning an astonishing income of $39,861 from his investments.[18]

Carnegie did his railroad job so well that in 1865, Pennsylvania Railroad President J. Edgar Thomson offered to promote him to general superintendent. Carnegie, however, declined. Just before the Civil War ended with Union victory in April 1865, he made an important personal decision—he quit the Pennsylvania Railroad.

5

INVESTOR AND INDUSTRIALIST

M y investments now began to require so much of my personal attention," Carnegie later admitted, "that I resolved to leave the service of the railway company and devote myself exclusively to my own affairs. . . . I was determined to make a fortune."[1]

By 1865, Carnegie had become a shrewd judge of investment opportunities, and he grabbed every good chance he could find. His Columbia Oil Company investment, for example, showed that Carnegie was willing to take risks.

In 1859, a group of business investors had hired Edwin Drake to drill an oil well near Titusville, Pennsylvania. For centuries, the local Seneca Indians

had skimmed oil from pools of water in the region and had used it for fuel and medicine. On August 27, 1859, Drake's drill struck oil, and his pump was soon drawing ten barrels of oil a day from the ground. Other adventurers rushed to Pennsylvania, hoping to make fortunes drilling for oil.

One of Carnegie's wealthy Homewood neighbors, William Coleman, sparked Carnegie's interest in oil. In the fall of 1861, Coleman and Carnegie traveled up the Allegheny River to visit the Pennsylvania oil fields. They bought a valuable piece of property, the Storey farm, for forty thousand dollars and organized the Columbia Oil Company. By 1862, the company was in full operation, producing over two thousand barrels of oil a day. Carnegie's daring investment earned him $17,868 in the first year alone. When a friend dropped by and asked him how he was doing, he exclaimed, "Oh, I'm rich, I'm rich!"[2]

The Pullman Palace Car Company

A rival sleeping-car company threatened the one Carnegie had formed with Theodore Woodruff. George Pullman had his own successful sleeping-car design. In the spring of 1867, the Woodruff and Pullman companies were competing to provide sleeping cars to the new western Union Pacific Railroad. Instead of fighting over patent rights in a court battle, Carnegie shrewdly chose to approach the problem differently. By chance, one summer

Colonel Edwin Drake (in top hat) stands in front of his oil well at Titusville, Pennsylvania. His success at pumping oil from the ground brought thousands of businessmen and speculators rushing to the oil fields of western Pennsylvania.

evening in 1869, Carnegie found himself mounting the grand marble stairway of the St. Nicholas Hotel in New York City side by side with Pullman.

"Good evening, Mr. Pullman," said Carnegie in his cheery manner. "How strange we should meet here." After a pause he continued, "Mr. Pullman, don't you think we are making nice fools of ourselves?" Quickly he pointed out that the rivalry between the two sleeping-car companies was helping no one but the railroads.

"Well," asked Pullman, "what do you suggest we do?"

"Unite!" declared Carnegie. "Let's make a joint proposition to the Union Pacific, your company and mine. Why not organize a new company to do it?"

"What would you call it?" asked Pullman suspiciously.

"The Pullman Palace Car Company," suggested Carnegie. Flattered to have the company named after him, Pullman agreed.[3] The Pullman Company, with Carnegie as its largest stockholder, soon gained almost complete control of the sleeping-car market worldwide.

The Keystone Bridge Company

"There were so many delays on railroads in those days from burned or broken wooden bridges," Carnegie would later explain, "that I felt the day of wooden bridges must end soon. . . . Cast iron bridges, I thought, ought to replace them, so I organized a company . . . and we called it the Keystone Bridge Company."[4] By the end of the Civil War, the Keystone Bridge Company had begun construction in earnest. With the powerful backing of the Pennsylvania Railroad, it became a most prosperous manufacturer of cast-iron railroad bridges.

The Keystone Bridge Company secured the contract to provide the iron beams and cables for the St. Louis Bridge across the Mississippi River. Construction began in 1868. On July 2, 1874,

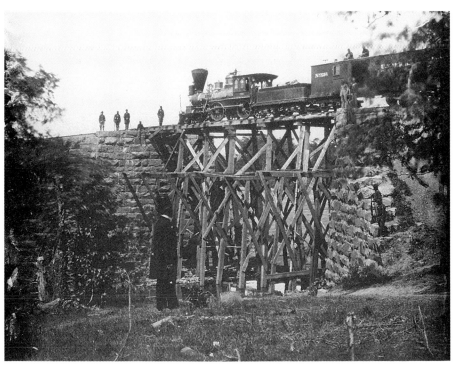

Wooden railroad bridges often collapsed or caught fire from the flying sparks of passing locomotive chimneys. Carnegie proposed to solve the problem by building bridges of cast iron.

This is a view of the St. Louis Bridge under construction. Its designer, Captain James B. Eads, was a former United States Army engineer.

General William T. Sherman drove the last spike connecting the bridge with the railroad line on the shore.[5] The bridge contained the longest iron beams ever manufactured in America. It was an engineering miracle, the largest iron arch bridge in the world at the time, with a total length of 1,524 feet.

Carnegie's Keystone Bridge Company became the leader in the United States bridge-building industry. Its cast-iron bridges were regarded as the strongest and safest. Other Keystone successes included the Missouri River bridge at Omaha, Nebraska; the Mississippi River bridge at Keokuk, Iowa; the Ohio River bridges at Cincinnati and at Point Pleasant, West Virginia; and a bridge across Raritan Bay in New Jersey.[6]

Keystone iron parts went into the main exhibition hall at the 1876 Centennial Exposition in Philadelphia. The company built bridges in Mexico and South America and a lighthouse at Tampico, Mexico.[7] Even the great Brooklyn Bridge in New York City, which was begun in 1869 and completed in 1883, used Keystone's iron and steel.

The Union Iron Mills

Carnegie quickly realized the value of iron, and in March 1865, he organized a new company, the Union Iron Mills. From 1865 to 1872, thirty-one thousand miles of new railroad track were laid across America.[8] The nation's bridges, locomotives, and sleeping cars all depended on iron, so Carnegie boldly began pouring all of his money into his iron

Miles of Bridges
If all the bridges built by the Keystone Bridge Company by 1883 had been placed end to end, they would have measured over thirty miles in length.

mills. "I determined," he explained, "that the proper policy was 'to put all good eggs in one basket and then watch that basket.'"[9]

On December 1, 1870, Carnegie and his Union Iron Mills partners began the construction of a blast furnace on Fifty-first Street in Pittsburgh. They named it the Lucy furnace, after Tom Carnegie's wife. Both the Lucy and a rival Pittsburgh furnace called the Isabella towered seventy-five feet high, and in the early summer of 1872, each furnace started producing fifty tons of iron a day.[10] Hardened in molds, the iron was called pig iron because each piece looked like a piglet. Carnegie encouraged the managers of the rival furnaces to compete in order to increase his output of iron.

Carnegie the Salesman

Late in the autumn of 1867, Carnegie had opened an office at 19 Broad Street in New York to promote his various interests. He and his mother moved into the St. Nicholas Hotel on Broadway. New York was the center of American business. Carnegie's boundless energy, his friendly good humor, and his absolute honesty gained him the trust of New York bankers and business leaders.

In the spring of 1872, President Thomson of the Pennsylvania Railroad commissioned Carnegie to go to Europe to sell a block of railroad bonds for a new railroad line to run to Davenport, Iowa. Carnegie sailed in April and successfully sold $6 million worth

These railroad tracks were destroyed by Union troops at Atlanta, Georgia, in 1864. The rebuilding of Southern railroads after the Civil War required tons of iron.

of bonds to European bankers. His commission on the sale amounted to $150,000.[11]

With his Scottish ancestry; his bright, open personality; and his excellent railroad connections, Carnegie was chosen by other United States railroad companies to sell bonds as well. His briefcase stuffed with bonds to sell, Carnegie voyaged back and forth across the Atlantic.

The Bessemer Converter

His trips to England brought Carnegie the idea of steel. In 1872, he first saw the volcanic, spectacular

eruption of a Bessemer converter during a visit to a British steel mill. Steel, an iron alloy, was stronger than iron. Iron railroad tracks wore out quickly under heavy train traffic. Rails on curves often had to be replaced. Carnegie remembered seeing as superintendent "new iron rails replaced every six weeks or two months . . . upon certain curves."[12] Steel rails, however, could last for years.

Steelmaking in America had increased in 1846 after William Kelly in Kentucky had discovered a new way of removing the impurities from iron at his iron forge. In England, Henry Bessemer had made similar experiments enabling cheaper steel production costs. Bessemer's process blasted compressed air through molten iron with a heat so intense it burned away all the impurities. At the same time, new iron-ore fields were being discovered in the upper peninsula of Michigan. The United States had the potential to become the greatest steel producer in the world.[13]

Carnegie realized steel would prove more useful than iron, not only in railroads but in ships, buildings, bridges, and machinery of all sorts. After seeing the Bessemer process in England, he rushed back to America. "The day of iron has passed," Carnegie exclaimed to his associates in the iron industry. "Steel is king!"[14]

6

THE STEEL KING

"My decision was taken early," Carnegie declared. "I would concentrate upon the manufacture of . . . steel and be master of that."[1] He returned from England in 1872, determined to build a great Bessemer steel mill. Carnegie persuaded friends and associates to invest in Carnegie, McCandless & Company. Carnegie put partner David McCandless's name in the company's title. His brother, Tom, and Tom's father-in-law, William Coleman, were also partners in the new venture. As a site for the new mill, they picked out 107 acres of farmland, called Braddock's Field, twelve miles southeast of Pittsburgh on the Monongahela River. The river, as well as the Pennsylvania Railroad and

the Baltimore and Ohio Railroad, offered easy transportation.

Carnegie hired Alexander L. Holley, America's foremost expert on Bessemer steelworks, to design the mill, supervise its construction, and get production started. Carnegie named the mill the Edgar Thomson Steel Works after the president of the Pennsylvania Railroad. He hoped that railroad would be a major customer.

The Edgar Thomson Steel Works, the largest and most modern steel mill in America, would consist of two five-ton Bessemer converters, a rolling mill, and a pair of five-ton Siemens open-hearth furnaces. There would be a gas-producing department, a boiler department, machine and smithy shops, a railroad, and a complete waterworks. Holley estimated that the mill would be able to produce thirty thousand tons of steel rails a year.[2]

The Panic of 1873

A financial panic shocked America in 1873 when Jay Cooke & Company, one of the country's largest

Historic Braddock's Field
Braddock's Field, the site of the Edgar Thomson Steel Works, was the spot where British General Edward Braddock's army, on its way to attack French Fort Duquesne, had been defeated during the colonial French and Indian War in 1755.

banks, suddenly failed. While the nation's credit tumbled, Carnegie brashly continued to build his steelworks. When he needed more money, he sold his shares in the Pullman Palace Car Company and his Western Union stock.

In the midst of the panic, Carnegie's old boss Thomas Scott presented him with more trouble. As a railroad developer, Scott had borrowed money for the construction of the Texas and Pacific Railroad. Now the banks wanted their loans guaranteed. In desperation, Scott begged Carnegie to provide him with the credit he needed. "It was one of the most trying moments of my whole life," Carnegie remembered. He could not allow himself to get involved with Scott's risky project. He had to protect his own interests. His refusal to help cost him Scott's friendship.[3]

Carnegie pushed ahead with the building of his steel mill. Manufacturers hungry for business agreed to supply necessary equipment at greatly reduced prices. Railroads offered to lower their freight rates for the transportation of supplies. Construction workers, glad to have jobs, worked cheaply, preparing the great mill. On August 6, 1875, the Edgar Thomson Steel Works received its first order—two thousand steel rails, from the Pennsylvania Railroad. On September 1, the mill produced its first rail.

Carnegie set about getting additional orders. He personally knew nearly every important railroad

official in America, and he sold his rails more cheaply than any other mill owner. He roamed far and wide seeking orders.

Captain William Jones in Charge

Carnegie hired the best workers he could find to run his steel mill. In the spring of 1873, a labor dispute had taken place at the Cambria Iron Works at Johnstown, Pennsylvania. Carnegie grabbed that opportunity to invite key workers at Cambria to come work at the Edgar Thomson mill. Captain William R. Jones agreed to become general super-intendent, and many other valued Cambria workers followed. In one bold stroke, Carnegie had hired over two hundred trained men who already knew how to make Bessemer steel.[4]

Captain Jones drove his workers hard, on twelve-hour shifts, even in the heat of summer when temperatures in the mill reached more than 100°F. Every day was a workday, Sunday included. But Jones also believed in making his workers com-fortable. He insisted that windows be provided for light and fresh air in the workshops. He made sure the work crews received breakfast each morning and had fresh water to drink all day. Jones loved his work, the heat of the blast furnaces, the noise of metal rolling over metal. By 1877, four blast fur-naces were in operation at the Edgar Thomson mill. Jones put the work crews in sporting competition with one another. The team with the largest weekly production could raise a giant steel broom high on their furnace's smoke stack as a proud trophy.[5]

Carnegie readily adopted Jones's "scrap-heap" policy at the mill. Instead of waiting until machinery wore out, the moment that an improvement was invented, the old machinery was dragged to the scrap heap, and the newest invention put in its place.[6] Jones personally invented a mixer for the mill. The Jones mixer was a huge, brick-lined iron box. It could hold half a million pounds of molten iron. The mixer, when rocked back and forth like a cradle, thoroughly mixed the liquid iron and made it uniform in quality. The Jones mixer greatly reduced the cost of making steel.

Making Steel

In order to make steel, workers shoveled trainloads of iron ore, coke (a baked form of coal), and crushed

Captain Jones's Workers
Captain William Jones had certain prejudices about the workers he hired. He once told Carnegie, "My experience has shown that Germans and Irish, Swedes, and . . . young American country boys . . . make the most effective . . . force you can find. Scotchmen do very well, are honest and faithful. Welsh can be used in limited numbers. But mark me, Englishmen have been the worst class of men I have had anything to do with."[7]

limestone into the blast furnaces, where intense heat separated the iron from the iron ore. Every so often the furnaces were "tapped," and the red-hot molten iron flowed into a train of bucket ladles. At every curve and bump of the moving train, some of the metal slopped over, spraying a galaxy of shooting stars. Presently, the train arrived alongside the Jones mixer, where the contents of the many ladles were mixed.[8]

Poured from the mixer, a second train of cars carried the liquid iron on to a Bessemer converter. The hot liquid was poured into the converter, and then a blast of air blew through small holes in the lower end of the huge iron pot. The flame at the mouth of the converter blew violet, then orange, and finally, pure white as the impurities were blown away, leaving liquid steel.

A worker then tilted the great pot sideways. Another shoveled in several hundred pounds of carbon mixture, to restore part of the lost carbon. Then the sputtering fluid was poured into molds. As soon as the steel had cooled into red-hot ingots, they were rushed to rollers to be squeezed into shape. The ingots plunged forward and backward through the rollers, becoming longer and thinner. Sparks sprayed into the air as the ingots were shaped into rails. Two whirling saws then cut off the rail ends with a sudden shriek and a blaze of fireworks. Steel grips flung the rails through a cold rolling machine

Molten steel is seen here pouring from a ladle into molds for cooling at the Edgar Thomson Steel Works.

for hardening. Final straightening and the drilling of spike holes completed the rail-making process.[9]

The Edgar Thomson Steel Works was so well arranged that it was practically one great machine. At one end stood the furnaces and ore piles. At the other end the steel bars dropped into the cooling pit at the rate of one per second, and the loaded freight cars rumbled noisily out of the yard.

Squeezing Profits

Tom Carnegie remained in Pittsburgh and ran the daily operations of the company. Andrew Carnegie spent much of his time selling the steel. He made good use of his close friendships with important rail-road men. Week after week he arrived at the office with a smile of victory and steel contracts bulging in his pockets. Still, he followed all developments at the mill closely. By 1878, Carnegie, McCandless & Company was producing more steel than any other company in the nation. "We broke all records for making steel last week," one manager proudly telegraphed Carnegie. "Congratulations!" Carnegie replied. "What about next week?" "No. 8 Furnace broke all records today," wired a blast-furnace supervisor. Carnegie wired back, "What were the others doing?"[10]

Carnegie constantly looked for ways to save money at the mill. "Show me your cost sheets" was his special slogan. Combing through the cost sheets, for example, Carnegie realized that fire insurance at the mill was so expensive that it would be cheaper to replace all of the wooden buildings with iron ones. He ordered it done and then canceled all his fire-insurance policies.[11]

Carnegie greatly relied on his chief bookkeeper, W. P. Shinn. Shinn insisted that every bit of raw material, waste material, and final product be weighed and accounted for. One day a workman engaged in building a heating furnace complained to a fellow worker, "There goes that . . . bookkeeper. If I use a dozen bricks more than I did last month, he knows it and comes round to ask why!" The smallest details in the cost of materials and labor in every department appeared from day to day in Shinn's accounts.[12]

Carnegie's partner Henry Phipps also saved the company money. Phipps discovered that the cinder waste material from the blast furnaces could be reused as fuel instead of thrown away. He also noticed that as the red-hot steel passed through the rollers, tiny shavings piled up on the floor. Phipps had the waste metal tested and found it was high-grade, useable steel. Phipps convinced Carnegie that the company needed a full-time chemist. Carnegie later explained, "We found . . . a learned German, Dr. Fricke, and great secrets did the doctor open up to us." As the company's chemist, Fricke tested the ores from various iron mines and advised Carnegie on which were the best to buy. Within his first year,

Dr. Fricke had earned his salary over and over again by saving the company money.[13]

Carnegie Brothers & Co.

"Our success was phenomenal," exclaimed Carnegie about his efficient company.[14] By 1877, the Edgar Thomson Steel Works were producing so much steel that Carnegie had more than was needed to fill rail orders. He began selling steel to Pittsburgh manufacturers of buggy springs and railroad-car axles, farmers' plows, stovepipe, and roofing gutters.

On the advice of Captain Jones, Carnegie began the eight-hour workday. "Flesh and blood cannot stand twelve hours' continuous work," Jones said.[15] The eight-hour shifts lasted from 1877 to 1888, when Carnegie was forced to return to the standard twelve-hour shifts in order to stay competitive with rival steelmakers.[16]

Grateful for Captain Jones's loyal service to the company, Carnegie offered to make him a partner. "No, Mr. Carnegie, I'm much obliged," Jones replied. "I don't know anything about business, and I don't want to be bothered with it. But," he suggested, "you can give me a hell of a big salary."

Carnegie declared that he would do it. He said, "After this, captain, you shall have the salary of the President of the United States—twenty-five thousand dollars."[17]

In 1881, Carnegie merged all his companies, including the Edgar Thomson Steel Works, the

This is Andrew Carnegie as he looked in the 1870s, a wealthy man of the world.

Union Iron Company, and the Keystone Bridge Company, into one big, new corporation. Carnegie Brothers & Co., was the largest company of its kind in the United States, and Carnegie owned 54.4 percent.

That same year, he bought a share of the Henry C. Frick Coke Company. Coke coal was essential in the making of steel. For each ton of iron ore smelted in a blast furnace, about half a ton of coke was burned. The best coal for making coke was found in south-western Pennsylvania, and Henry Clay Frick owned most of those coalfields. In time, Carnegie bought a majority interest in the Frick Coke Company in order to guarantee his mills a steady supply of coke at a fixed price.

Another wise move was Carnegie's purchase of a rival mill called the Homestead in October 1883. The brand-new Homestead Works, located a mile downriver from the Edgar Thomson mill, had the most modern equipment available. Because the owners were having financial difficulties, Carnegie could buy the mill at a bargain price. The Homestead Works provided steel beams for the first skyscraper office building in America, the Home Insurance Building in Chicago. Carnegie steel beams also went into the Washington Monument and new elevated railroads in New York and Chicago.

In 1873, the first full year of operation, the Edgar Thomson mill had produced 21,674 tons of steel. In 1889, it would produce a stunning 536,838 tons. Carnegie's bold determination to put most of his company's profits back into new equipment, rather than pay dividends, often worried his partners. But his simple business policy was to first, "Cut the prices; scoop the market; run the mills full" and second, "Watch the costs and the profits will take care of themselves."[18]

7

MAN OF THE WORLD

An ocean voyage is good fun," Carnegie once declared.[1] He became a lifelong lover of travel after he took his trip back to Scotland in 1862. In May 1865, he happily sailed off with childhood friends Henry Phipps and John Vandevort on a tour of Europe. For nine months, they traveled with knapsacks on their backs through Great Britain, Holland, Germany, and France. They hiked dusty country roads and climbed mountain peaks. They visited many of Europe's great cities and went to museums, cathedrals, plays, and operas.

As Carnegie's wealth increased, he began to travel more often. In October 1878, he embarked on a trip around the world with his friend John

Vandevort. From San Francisco, they set sail for Japan aboard the S.S. *Belgic*. "I'm off for a holiday," he declared in his travel diary, "and the rise and fall of iron and steel affecteth me not."[2]

From Japan they journeyed to China, then on to India and Egypt. In China, Carnegie read Confucius. In India, he read Buddha. Based on his readings in foreign religion and philosophy, as well as on his observations, Carnegie came to believe that every people and culture had something of value to teach. During his travels, he grew to understand that "No nation has all that is best, neither is any [without] some advantages."[3]

On March 20, 1879, Carnegie and Vandevort arrived in the Bay of Naples on the coast of Italy. "Early morning!" Carnegie wrote in his diary. "Yes my dear friends, it is round. Here stands Mount Vesuvius in full view this morning, making for itself pure white clouds of steam, which float in the otherwise clear, cloudless sky. . . ."[4] The tour around the world ended with a coach trip through England and Scotland. For the long days at sea, Carnegie enjoyed reading a complete set of the plays of Shakespeare, making notes and memorizing passages. After a trip of 243 days, the two travelers finally arrived home in New York.

The Habits of a Rich Man

After his world trip, Carnegie often chose to spend his summer months in Scotland, England, or mainland Europe. He also spent time with his mother at

Braemar Cottage in Cresson, Pennsylvania. Since his heat exhaustion in 1862, he had felt the need to go someplace cool during the hot months. Braemar Cottage, high in the Allegheny Mountains, fifty miles east of Pittsburgh, was the perfect escape.

In New York in the winters, Carnegie attended the theater, art galleries, the opera, and other social events. He also engaged private tutors in order to study literature, history, philosophy, economics, and French. He wished to make up for his missing school years. The brash steelmaker also joined the Nineteenth Century Club, an exclusive group of New Yorkers who met to discuss the important issues of the day. As Carnegie became a famous manufacturer, he made friendships with intellectuals and statesmen such as philosophers Herbert Spencer and Matthew Arnold, British Prime Minister William Gladstone, and Civil War General William Tecumseh Sherman.

With opinions on a broad range of subjects, he also became one of the most popular and sought-after speakers of his day. Though he had never grown taller than five feet three inches, on the public platform Carnegie was a dramatic showman. "Frequently rising to his tiptoes and pumping his short arms vigorously," an observer recalled, "he looked like a bantam rooster ready to crow."[5] Carnegie used the speaking skills he had learned as a young man debating above Phipps's cobbling shop.

A Return to Dunfermline

Once, as a boy in Allegheny, Carnegie saw his mother crying because of her hard life. He had grasped her hands and promised, "Someday I'll be rich, and we'll ride in a fine coach driven by four horses." His mother only wept and said, "That will do no good over here, if no one in Dunfermline can see us."[6]

In 1881, Carnegie kept his promise and fulfilled her dreams. In England, he purchased a great coach and hired a coachman, footman, and a handsome team of four horses. Then, with his mother and nine of their friends, he set out from Brighton, on England's southern coast, for a grand, seven-week trip north to Scotland.[7]

On June 17, 1881, the coach wheeled away from the Grand Hotel at Brighton and headed north. "All seated!" Carnegie later described. "Mother next the coachman, and I at her side. The horn sounds, the crowd cheers, and we are off." The coach bounced along country roads and through old English market towns. Carnegie gleefully wrote in his diary,

> No mode of travel [can] be compared with coaching. By all other modes the views are obstructed by hedges and walls; upon the top of the coach the eye wanders far and wide. . . . Everything of rural England is seen, and how exquisitely beautiful it all is, this quiet, peaceful, orderly land!

The travelers slowly rolled northward through Guildford, Reading, Oxford, Banbury Cross, and Stratford-upon-Avon, spending the nights at country

inns and dining at noon, picnic style, in country meadows.[8]

After leaving Coventry on June 24, the coaching party entered the "Black Country" of England's industrial Midlands. Carnegie wrote, "We see the Black Country now, rows of little dingy houses beyond, with tall smokey chimneys vomiting smoke, mills and factories at every turn, coal pits and rolling mills and blast furnaces. . . . it is just Pittsburgh over again. . . ."[9]

They crossed the border into Scotland on July 16. "The bridge across the boundary-line was . . . reached," Carnegie described:

> When midway over a halt was called, and vent given to our enthusiasm. With three cheers for the land of the heather, shouts of "Scotland forever," and the waving of hats and handkerchiefs, we dashed across the border. O Scotland, my own, my native land, your exiled son returns. . . .[10]

Nine days later, the coach rolled into Dunfermline, past banners reading, "Welcome Carnegie, generous son." The whole town had turned out to greet the famous steelmaker. The city held a parade, eight thousand marchers strong, a great procession of workers' guilds and unions. Five brass bands blared Scottish tunes, and bystanders cheered and waved as Carnegie's coach passed by. The Carnegie family had fled from Dunfermline in poverty thirty-three years before. But now Margaret Carnegie had returned in a magnificent coach, to the joyful shouts and applause of the whole city.

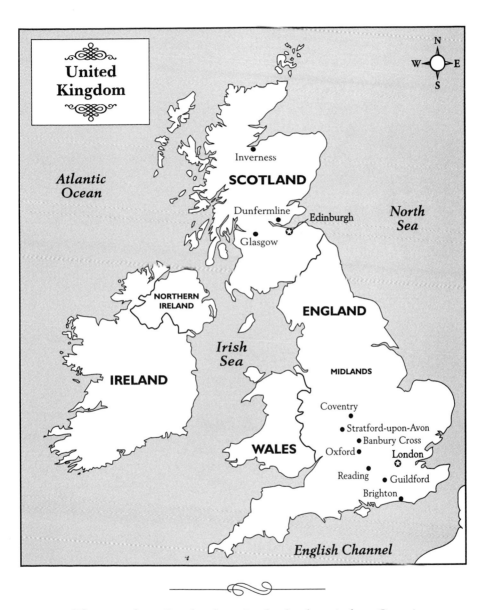

This map shows Dunfermline, Scotland, where Andrew Carnegie was born, as well as some of the places he visited on his 1881 stagecoach trip with his mother from Brighton, England, to Inverness, Scotland.

For her, the greatest moment of the Dunfermline visit was when she ceremonially cemented the foundation stone of a new free public library that her son was donating to the town.

On August 3, the coaching party reached Inverness on Scotland's northern coast. It marked the end of the 831-mile trip that neither Carnegie nor his mother would ever forget.

Taking Time for Romance

In 1880, at the age of forty-five, Carnegie had become acquainted with a twenty-four-year-old woman named Louise Whitfield. Whitfield was the daughter of a fairly well-to-do New York City merchant. She lived on West Forty-eighth Street, not far from the Windsor Hotel where Carnegie was living with his mother. Both Carnegie and Whitfield enjoyed horseback riding and got to know each other while riding in Central Park. In time, their friendship blossomed into romance. By 1883, they seemed to be engaged, but then they agreed simply to remain close friends. She was, after all, twenty-one years younger than Carnegie, and Margaret Carnegie, a possessive mother, refused to give up her son.

Newspaperman and Writer

As a young man, Carnegie was proud to have letters describing his 1865 European trip printed in the *Pittsburgh Commercial* newspaper. Sometimes he dreamed of becoming a full-time newspaper writer and publisher. In 1881, while visiting Great Britain, Carnegie decided to finance a whole chain of liberal newspapers.

With Carnegie's support, a chain of eighteen newspapers was created, centered mainly in the industrial cities of northern England. He hired editors interested in promoting social and economic reforms in Great Britain. Carnegie, with his Chartist background, still wanted an end to royalty and a much more representative form of government in Great Britain. In time, though, he realized his newspapers would not succeed unless he gave them his full attention. Therefore, he sold his interest in some of the papers and gave away his interest in others to their editors.

Carnegie enjoyed greater success as a writer of books. In 1880, he published *Round the World*, describing his global trip with John Vandevort. In energetic style, he leaped joyfully into his story: "New York, Saturday, Oct. 12, 1878. Bang! click! the desk closes, the key turns, and good-by for a year."[11]

After his coach trip through Great Britain in 1881, he had an account privately printed and given to friends. A New York publisher suggested bringing out an edition for sale to the public. Carnegie titled his second book *An American Four-In-Hand in Britain*. In the British edition, the book began in almost exactly the same way as *Round the World*:

"Bang! click! once more the desk closes and the key turns! Not 'Round the World' again, but 'Ho for England, for England!' is the cry, and 'Scotland's hills and Scotland's dales and Scotland's vales for me.'"[12]

In 1886, Carnegie's *Triumphant Democracy*, his most serious and widely read book, was published. The book warmly praised America's opportunities and achievements. Carnegie still hoped to persuade the British to embrace the American system of government. "The old nations of the earth creep on at a snail's pace," Carnegie insisted, while the United States "thunders past with the rush of an express."[13]

"Wealth"

Carnegie published dozens of magazine articles in his lifetime about his travels and his thoughts on business. In 1889, he published an article in the American magazine *The North American Review*. Called simply "Wealth," the article touched upon the duty of millionaires to distribute their wealth during their lifetimes. "The man who dies . . . rich dies disgraced," Carnegie bluntly declared.[14]

Carnegie himself had already donated a swimming pool to Dunfermline in 1873. In 1881, he had given Dunfermline a public library. He had also built a library in Braddock, Pennsylvania. He had donated an organ to his father's church in Allegheny and had given six thousand dollars to the University of Western Pennsylvania (now the University of

Built in 1879, the Carnegie Free Library in Allegheny, Pennsylvania (now part of Pittsburgh), was one of Carnegie's earliest philanthropic gifts.

Pittsburgh).[15] In 1885, he gave fifty thousand dollars to establish the first medical research laboratory in the United States, at Bellevue Hospital in New York. He also paid to send four small children to Paris, to be treated by Louis Pasteur for rabies—the first Americans to receive that treatment.[16] Carnegie had begun his career as a philanthropist.

8

Tragedy and Triumph

A m keeping in the house and hope to be all
right. . . . Yours miserably, A.C."[1] Carnegie
wrote this note to Louise Whitfield in early October
1886. He had a bad cold. He was at the summer
house in Cresson, Pennsylvania, watching over his
mother, who at the age of seventy-six had developed
pneumonia. At the same time, his brother, Tom, lay
seriously ill with pneumonia in Pittsburgh.

For two weeks, Carnegie remained in bed, and
finally the doctors diagnosed his case as typhoid
fever. His illness worsened when he learned that
Tom had died. For four more weeks, Carnegie hov-
ered between life and death in his darkened room in
Cresson. When his mother died on November 10,

his doctors and servants kept the heartbreaking news from him for a week. The undertakers lowered his mother's coffin out her bedroom window so that it would not have to pass his sickroom door.

Slowly Carnegie's health improved. Late in November he felt strong enough to scribble a note to Louise Whitfield. "Louise, I am now wholly yours— all gone but you. . . . Till death, Louise, yours alone."[2] On April 22, 1887, Andrew Carnegie and Louise Whitfield married in New York City. Carnegie was fifty-one and Whitfield was thirty. They honeymooned on the Isle of Wight off the coast of England.

The Rise of Henry Clay Frick

With the death of Tom Carnegie, an important position became vacant at Carnegie Brothers & Co. In January 1889, Carnegie chose Henry Clay Frick to become the new chief executive officer. Frick, who had built a fortune in Pennsylvania's coalfields, became Carnegie's most determined and effective manager. "Take supreme care of that head of yours," Carnegie wrote to Frick. "It is wanted. Again, expressing my thankfulness that I have found THE MAN, I am always yours, A.C."[3]

Frick's first great success after assuming the leadership of Carnegie Brothers & Co., was the inexpensive purchase of a rival steelworks at Duquesne, Pennsylvania. Duquesne was one of the most modern and best-equipped steelworks in the country. Once Duquesne was bought, Frick streamlined

Carnegie's company. On July 1, 1892, Carnegie Brothers officially became the Carnegie Steel Company, the largest steel company in the world. It included four major steel mills—the Edgar Thomson, the Homestead, the Duquesne, and the Hartman—as well as the Upper and Lower Iron Mills, the Lucy Furnaces, the Keystone Bridge Company, the Scotia mines, and the Larimer and Yonghiogheny coke works.[4] Frick assembled these units into a perfectly balanced organization. The company owned its own iron mines, steamships, harbors, railroads, and blast furnaces. From the moment the iron ore was dug out of the earth until it flowed in a stream of molten steel into the mill ladles, there was never a fee paid to an outsider.[5]

Under Frick's leadership, profits rose from $2 million in 1888 to $3.5 million in 1889 to $5.4 million in 1890. Carnegie looked to the future with confidence. He had a private fortune worth $30 million and an income of $2 million a year.[6]

The Homestead Strike

In 1892, one of the worst episodes in American labor history suddenly erupted. That July, Carnegie's contract with union workers at the Homestead Works was due to be renewed. Out of the more than 3,800 men employed at Homestead, 325 were members of the Amalgamated Association of Iron and Steel Workers.

Carnegie had always paid his workers fairly. He believed industry should be a partnership between the employer and the employees. According to Carnegie's "sliding scale" wage plan, the pay of all the workers normally rose or dropped according to company profits.[7] But Carnegie went to Scotland in the spring of 1892. He left Frick in charge of the latest Homestead contract negotiations. While Carnegie vacationed at remote Rannoch Lodge, Frick ordered a stockade built around the Homestead Works, complete with watchtowers, rifle slits, and a high board fence topped with barbed wire. In addition, Frick secretly requested that the Pinkerton Detective Agency prepare to send three hundred guards. Frick felt no sympathy for the workers, and he believed he could force them to accept his contract offer. On July 1, more than thirty-five hundred disgruntled Homestead employees went on strike. The great mill at Homestead fell dark.

On the hot night of July 5, 1892, two darkened barges carrying Pinkerton guards were towed quietly up the Monongahela River. Some Homestead strikers spotted the barges and rushed ahead to spread the news. The shrieks of sirens and factory whistles awakened the sleeping town of Homestead. Strikers and their wives and children hurried down to the riverbank. Many carried rifles and revolvers.

Strikers tore a gap in the wooden fence surrounding the mill and swept into the grounds. When

Henry Clay Frick (1849–1919), with his tough attitude toward the steel union, sparked the bloody Homestead strike of 1892.

the barges tied up at the company wharf at four o'clock in the morning on July 6, the strikers opened fire and the Pinkerton guards fired back. As bullets whizzed through the air, the towing tugboat steamed away, leaving the Pinkertons stranded on the barges.[8]

The angry crowd at the water's edge shouted taunts and threats and fired more gunshots. The Pinkertons crouched inside the barges and shot back. Two strikers fell dead, and several more clutched at painful wounds. A number of the Pinkerton men were injured, one of them fatally wounded.[9]

Strikers erected protective barricades of steel billets and beams in the mill yard. Throughout the day, they tried to kill the stranded Pinkertons. A railroad car loaded with oil and set on fire was rolled down a track toward the barges, but it derailed and stopped short. Strikers fired the town's courthouse cannon at the barges, but the old cannon exploded, taking off the head of a striker. They poured oil on the river and set fire to it, but the wind blew it the wrong way. A lighted stick of dynamite landed on a barge, but it splashed into a bucket of water. Inside the cramped barges, the air was stifling hot. Riflemen fired on any Pinkerton who ventured near a window or doorway for a gasp of fresh air.

Someone on the barges waved a white handkerchief, but the enraged strikers only fired another volley of bullets. Eyewitness Myron R. Stowell crouched among the strikers. "They only shot

when[ever] they saw something," he recalled, "and every crack of a rifle meant an attempt on a human life."[10] After twelve hours of fighting, five workers lay dead and many others were seriously wounded. One Pinkerton guard had been killed and eleven more were badly hurt.

At last, around four o'clock in the afternoon, the Pinkerton guards, fearing for their lives, again raised a white flag. Strike leader Hugh O'Donnell went aboard and promised the Pinkertons safe conduct out of town if they would surrender. The frightened Pinkertons agreed. They dropped their guns, jumped off the barges, and waded ashore. But O'Donnell discovered he could not control the furious mob. For nearly a mile the Pinkertons had to run a gauntlet past screaming and cursing men, women, and children. Strikers beat the hated "Pinks" with stockings filled with iron scraps, gouged at their eyes with pointed umbrellas, threw sand and dirt in their faces, and kicked them when they fell. At every step, the defenseless guards were struck with fists, clubs, and stones. Three more Pinkerton guards were killed, and every one of them suffered before he reached safety.[11]

Order Restored

On July 12, the governor of Pennsylvania called out eight thousand National Guard troops to restore order and protect the Homestead mill. Still, the violence was not over. A Lithuanian immigrant named

Defeated Pinkerton guards walk toward the terrible gauntlet. This drawing appeared in Frank Leslie's Illustrated *magazine soon after the Homestead strike.*

Alexander Berkman, an anarchist, blamed Frick for the Homestead tragedy. On July 23, Berkman burst into Frick's office and fired shots at him with a pistol. Blood spurted from two wounds in Frick's neck, as Berkman was wrestled to the floor by company Vice President J. G. A. Leishman. Even then, Berkman managed to stab Frick three times in the hips and legs with a dagger before startled office workers dragged him away.

When the bullets were removed and his bleeding wounds bandaged, Frick insisted on returning to his desk. He wrote out a telegram to Carnegie in which he exclaimed, "I am still in shape to fight the battle out." To the newspapers, Frick announced, "I will fight this thing to the bitter end. I will never recognize the union, never, never!"[12]

Carnegie was stunned when he learned of the bloodshed at Homestead. He cabled Frick, "Never employ one of these rioters. Let grass grow over the works. . . ."[13] Although Berkman was not connected with the steelworkers' union, his murder attempt turned many people against the Homestead strikers. During the next two months, Frick hired outsiders to start up the mill again. Some regular workers, their spirits broken and hungry for wages, also returned to work. By November 1892, the strike had ended. Three fifths of the striking Homestead workers had lost their jobs.

Many newspapers accused Andrew Carnegie of hiding out in Scotland during the conflict. The public blamed him for the tragedy. The *St. Louis Post-Dispatch* commented:

> Three months ago Andrew Carnegie was a man to be envied. Today he is an object of mingled pity and contempt. . . . A single word from him might have saved the bloodshed—but the word was never spoken. . . . Say what you will of Frick, he is a brave man. Say what you will of Carnegie, he is a coward.[14]

Carnegie would later sadly write of the tragedy, "Nothing I have ever had to meet in all my life, before or since, wounded me so deeply. No pangs remain of any wound received in my business career save that of Homestead. It was so unnecessary."[15] The Homestead strike had broken the steelworkers' union, and Carnegie was glad of that. However, it had also destroyed his reputation as a friend to the workers.

Building an Empire

Carnegie never fully trusted Frick again. In December 1894, he forced Frick to step aside as chief operating executive of Carnegie Steel. Frick would serve instead as chairman of the board, a mostly honorary position. Now Carnegie looked elsewhere for company leadership. In just five years, Charles Schwab had risen from a common laborer to become the superintendent of the Homestead mill. Carnegie made Schwab president of the company. When Schwab cut costs by reducing labor

expenses, improving production methods, and negotiating better business contracts, Carnegie exalted, "You are a hustler. . . . I am rejoicing at your brilliant success."[16]

Through the 1890s, Carnegie continued to expand his holdings. He realized the importance of owning and controlling everything needed to make steel. The Mesabi Range was a rich new deposit of iron ore discovered in Minnesota in 1891. Instead of being dug from deep mines, the ore lay near the surface of the ground. Giant steam shovels could scoop it up easily. It cost five cents a ton to dig Mesabi ore, as opposed to three dollars a ton for underground ore.[17]

Carnegie bought the rights to many of the new Minnesota iron-ore fields. He leased the rights to others from millionaire John D. Rockefeller at bargain prices simply because he could promise to use 1.2 million tons of ore every year for fifty years. *Iron Age* magazine called it Carnegie's greatest achievement: "It gives the Carnegie Company a position unequaled by any steel producer in the world."[18]

In 1898, Carnegie built a fleet of steamboats to bring the ore from Lake Superior to Conneaut, Ohio, a harbor he built on Lake Erie. He also built his own railroad line from the harbor to his Pittsburgh mills. By the end of 1899, Carnegie, in partnership with his boyhood friend Henry Oliver, controlled thirty-four iron mines and an efficient transportation system to bring iron ore to his mills.[19]

The Pinnacle of Success

There would always be a market for replacement rails, but by the 1890s, most of America's great railroads had already been built. Carnegie looked for new places to sell steel. The invention of the elevator made steel beams useful in the construction of multistoried city structures. Carnegie also found a growing market for steel in beams, braces, and plates for city elevated railroads. Farm tractors and machinery, barbed wire, and irrigation pipes required steel. He began to manufacture steel for great boilers, generators, and power turbines; shafts, axles, and wheels; and heavy armor plate for navy ships. Partner Henry Phipps pleaded with Carnegie, "By all means do let us go a little slower, my heart is often in my mouth when I read of [your] rushing way in *big* things."[20] But Carnegie's enthusiasm for new projects could not be stopped. Before long, half of Carnegie's steel production consisted of beams for skyscrapers; girders for elevated railroads; pipes for gas, water, and sewage; and other finished products. In 1898, Carnegie announced, "The next step—and it is coming, is to go into the manufacture of finished articles. . . . The concern that does this first will finish first."[21] Instead of just making raw steel, he wanted to manufacture finished railroad cars, wire, nails, and boilers himself.

Efficiency and reinvestment brought Carnegie Steel a flood of profits:

1895 . . . $5 million
1896 . . . $6 million
1897 . . . $7 million
1898 . . . $11.5 million
1899 . . . $21 million[22]

Only one thing gave him greater joy. After ten years of marriage, on March 30, 1897, Louise Carnegie had given birth to a daughter. They named the baby Margaret after Carnegie's mother. At the age of sixty-two, Carnegie became a father for the first time.

Rising to the Latest Challenge

In December 1899, Carnegie asked Henry Clay Frick to step down as chairman of the board. They had been fighting over the price of coke that the Frick Coke Company was to charge the Carnegie Steel Company. The feud soon became national news when Carnegie refused to pay Frick the full value of Frick's 11 percent interest in Carnegie Steel. In the sensational lawsuit that followed, the finances of the Carnegie Steel Company became public for the first time.[23] In the end, Frick was forced out as an officer of the company, but he won $15 million as a result of the lawsuit.

It was at this time that Frick and Henry Phipps tried to put together a deal to buy out Carnegie's interests. To Carnegie's grim satisfaction, the team of investment partners Frick and Phipps gathered could not raise the purchase price of $57 million

Steel wire, steel rods, and other steel products pile up in the yard of a Carnegie factory while awaiting shipment.

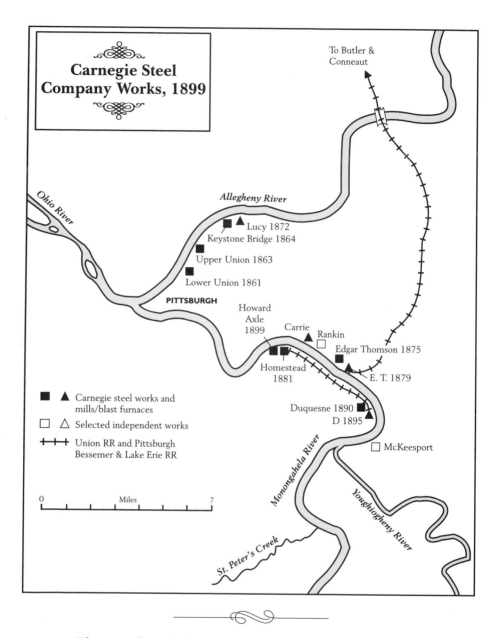

*This map shows the locations of some of the different branches of
Carnegie Steel in the Pittsburgh area in 1899.*

Carnegie demanded. When the deal fell through, Carnegie happily kept the $1.17 million deposit the investors had guaranteed him whether the deal went through or not.

In 1900, Carnegie Steel production reached an astounding 3 million tons. The company employed more than twenty thousand workers and shipped more steel than any other company in the world, seven hundred thousand tons more than the entire production of Great Britain. Company profits reached $40 million that year, and to compete with rival companies, Carnegie prepared to expand his steel empire even further. It was at that crucial moment that banker J. P. Morgan stepped in and made his offer. Morgan and his partners would pay $480 million for the Carnegie Steel Company. Carnegie agreed.

The Frick Collection

When Henry Clay Frick died in 1919, his will provided for the establishment of an art museum in his mansion at Seventieth Street and Fifth Avenue in New York City. Today the public can walk through the great halls and rooms of the mansion and view art from Frick's collection, including famous oil paintings by old masters such as Goya, El Greco, Rembrandt, and Vermeer, as well as beautiful Impressionist paintings by such artists as Degas, Monet, Renoir, and Whistler.

As boldly as he had built his business, Carnegie chose to give it up. At the age of sixty-five, with a private fortune of more than $360 million, he abruptly quit steelmaking. After the contracts with Morgan were signed, Carnegie excitedly stated, "Now Pierpont, I am the happiest man in the world."[24]

9

THE GREAT
PHILANTHROPIST

H urrah! I am out of business," Carnegie
exclaimed in 1901.[1] With his first gift of
twenty-five thousand dollars for a public swimming
pool to Dunfermline in 1873, Carnegie had begun
his career as a philanthropist. Now he was determined to do good things with the rest of his huge
fortune. "I'm not going to grow old piling up," he
insisted, "but in distributing."[2]

In 1901, the Carnegies moved into a grand new
mansion on the corner of Fifth Avenue and Ninety-
first Street in New York City. Carnegie made this
home the headquarters for his American philan-
thropies. In his magnificent library-study on the first
floor stood a rolltop desk so big that it had to be

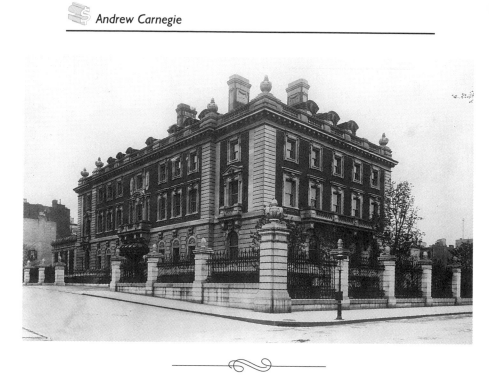

This is the Carnegie mansion at Ninety-first Street and Fifth Avenue in New York City. All of its structural beams were made of Carnegie steel.

constructed inside the room. There Carnegie sat, his feet barely able to touch the floor, deciding how best to dispose of his wealth.[3]

Every day's mail brought him a flood of letters from people requesting aid for themselves or support for some project in which they were interested. James Bertram, Carnegie's private secretary, guessed that Carnegie received as many as four hundred to five hundred letters each day. Carnegie's friend, the writer Mark Twain, sent one amusing request: "You seem to be in prosperity. Could you lend an admirer a dollar & a half to buy a hymn book with? God will bless you. I feel it. I know it. . . . P.S. Don't send the hymn-book, send the money. I want to make the selection myself."[4]

The makers of Mother Seigel's Syrup sponsored a contest called "How Mr. Carnegie Should Get Rid of His Wealth." Thousands of people responded with suggestions. Many begged for money for themselves. Some suggested that Carnegie give gifts to churches and to the poor. Others suggested that he pay for the free distribution of Mother Seigel's Syrup. Some thought he should give his fortune to his daughter, Margaret. A few thought he should pay off the national debt.[5]

Carnegie made one of his first major gifts in 1901. The Carnegie Trust for the Universities of Scotland was established with his gift of $10 million to aid four Scottish universities.[6]

The Cooper-Hewitt National Design Museum
Andrew Carnegie's mansion on Fifth Avenue consisted of sixty-four rooms on six floors. Today it houses the Cooper-Hewitt National Design Museum, part of the Smithsonian Institution. Visitors can stroll through the rooms, viewing exhibits of historic American furniture and household items, or sit in the garden where Carnegie so often enjoyed relaxing.

Building Libraries

Carnegie loved free public libraries and the knowledge they contained. He was determined to build more of them. He declared, "I believe that it outranks any other one thing that a community can do to benefit its people. It is the never failing spring in the desert."[7] In 1901, he gave $5.2 million to New York City for sixty-five libraries and $1 million to the city of St. Louis for the construction of libraries there.[8] "If one [child] in each library district, by having access to one of these libraries, is half as much benefited as I was by having access to Colonel Anderson's four hundred well-worn volumes," Carnegie said, "I shall consider they have not been established in vain."[9]

If a town pledged to provide a site and to buy books and maintain the new library building, Carnegie most often would agree to help. Over the entrance to each library, he suggested there be a representation of the rays of a rising sun, and the words "LET THERE BE LIGHT."[10] By the time of his death, Carnegie had given the money to build 2,811 free public libraries, of which 1,946 were located in the United States; 660 in Great Britain, including Ireland; 156 in Canada; 23 in New Zealand; 13 in South Africa; 6 in the British West Indies; 4 in Australia; and 1 each in the islands of Seychelles, Mauritius, and Fiji. The total cost for these libraries was $50,364,808. Every state in the

Union except for Rhode Island had at least one Carnegie library.[11]

Pension Funds, Hero Funds, and Organs

In the spring of 1901, Carnegie put aside $4 million to support employees and the families of employees of the Carnegie Steel Company who had been injured or killed at work. He also established old-age pensions for his former workers. "I made this first use of surplus wealth upon retiring from business," Carnegie explained, "as an acknowledgement of the deep debt I owe to the workmen who have contributed so greatly to my success."[12]

Without publicity, Carnegie supported many people with private pensions, ranging from friends in Dunfermline to such celebrities as writer Rudyard Kipling and educator Booker T. Washington. His pensioners included two ladies with whom Carnegie had once danced as a young man, a boyhood friend who had once held Carnegie's books while he ran a race, and a poor Pittsburgh mechanic to whom he had once delivered a telegram.[13]

When Carnegie learned that United States college professors rarely earned more than four hundred dollars a year, with no provisions for retirement, he decided to do something about it. After all, simple office clerks at Carnegie Steel had earned as much as that. In 1905, he established the Carnegie Teachers Pension Fund with $10 million. Originally, fifty-two colleges were accepted for

admission into this pension plan. As other colleges agreed to admit students of all religions, so they could join the plan as well, Carnegie added $5 million to the fund.

Carnegie established the Hero Fund in 1904 with an endowment of $5 million. "It is the fund that may be considered my pet," he stated.[14] The Hero Fund awarded medals and pensions to brave people for deeds of heroism. Hero Funds were established in the United States, Great Britain, France, Germany, Norway, Switzerland, the Netherlands, Sweden, Denmark, Belgium, and Italy.

The donation of church organs was another special Carnegie project. By 1919, Carnegie had given organs to 4,092 churches in the United States; 2,119 in England; 1,005 in Scotland; and an additional 473 throughout the rest of the world, at a cost of $6,248,312. In a grand total of 7,689 churches, the resounding notes of those pipe organs could be heard on Sundays.[15]

Other Carnegie Gifts

Carnegie established the Carnegie Institution in Washington, D.C., in 1904: "To encourage in the broadest and most liberal manner investigations, research and discovery, and the application of knowledge to the improvement of mankind."[16] During its first year, the institution founded departments in experimental evolution, marine biology, history, economics, and sociology. Later, departments were set up for the study of earthly magnetism, astronomy (at the Mount Wilson Observatory in California), geophysics, botany, nutrition, and other subjects. Carnegie took special delight in the work of the sailing ship *Carnegie*. The *Carnegie* was built with bronze parts instead of iron. Its magnetic compass gave extremely accurate readings, enabling the ship to sail far and wide, correcting nautical charts. "The *Carnegie* is going over all the seas year after year," Carnegie happily declared, "putting the world right."[17]

In Pittsburgh, Carnegie built the Carnegie Institute, with a library, museum, music hall, and art institute. In New York City, Carnegie's money paid for Carnegie Hall, a concert hall that today is world famous. The Carnegie Institute of Technology and the Margaret Morrison Carnegie College for women in Pittsburgh received $7.25 million from Carnegie. Among the other schools that received large gifts from Carnegie were Berea College, the Hampton Institute, and the Tuskegee Institute. These schools appealed to Carnegie's sense of justice. Berea was a college for youths from the mountains of Kentucky. African-American youths from the rural South attended Hampton and Tuskegee. At all three colleges, the students worked on campus to help pay for their educations.[18]

An Unusual Gift

Perhaps Carnegie's most unusual gift was the one he gave to New Jersey's Princeton University in 1906. At a cost of four hundred thousand dollars, workers dug a lake on the campus three and a half miles long, so Princeton students could enjoy the sport of rowing.[19]

Carnegie at Play

"Pity the poor millionaire," Carnegie once declared, "for the way of the philanthropist is hard."[20] During his first ten years as a philanthropist, he gave away $180 million. But he discovered he still had $180 million. So he created the Carnegie Corporation of New York in November 1911. To that corporation he transferred the bulk of his remaining fortune, $125 million, with the instructions:

> to promote the advancement . . . of knowledge among the people of the United States by aiding technical schools, institutions of higher lerning [*sic*], libraries, scientific reserch [*sic*], hero funds, useful publications, and by such other agencies and means as shall from time to time be found appropriate therefor [*sic*].[21]

For pleasure, Carnegie spent more time than ever in his beloved Scotland. Since 1888, the Carnegies had rented Cluny Castle north of Dunfermline in Scotland's central Highlands. Each summer, among mountains, lakes, and trout streams, the Carnegies enjoyed country life in grand style.

Andrew Carnegie, steel king and philanthropist. Even late in life he loved books and learning.

With the birth of their daughter in 1897, Louise Carnegie had proposed that the family get its own summer home in Scotland. Carnegie's realtors found an ancient estate known as Skibo, on the coast of northern Scotland, which included fifty square miles of property, complete with lakes, forests, trails, and streams. The castle needed many repairs and Carnegie put an army of builders to work. When finished, Skibo Castle became the Carnegies' home during the warm months of every year.

At Skibo, Carnegie kept guests occupied with fishing, hiking, and riding horseback or in carriages. In the evenings, he held parties, concerts, and lively discussions. At Skibo, Carnegie worked hard, played hard, and slept well. He exercised regularly and especially enjoyed golf. "I am so busy working at fun," he wrote his cousin Dod. "Fishing, yachting, golfing. Skibo never so delightful, all so quiet! A home at last."[22]

Skibo had a staff of eighty-five servants. A Scottish piper in full Highland dress awakened guests with bagpipe music each morning. The castle organ played during breakfast. Each Fourth of July, Carnegie hosted a grand party with spectacular fireworks. His British friends liked to call him "the star-spangled Scotchman."[23]

It gave Carnegie special joy when he purchased the entire Pittencrieff Estate in Dunfermline on Christmas Eve, 1902. As a boy, Carnegie had been prohibited from entering the estate because of his family's political views. To his cousin Dod, he now simply wrote, "Pittencrieff is ours."[24] For the first time in years, Carnegie and his relatives could set foot on the property. Carnegie opened Pittencrieff as a park.

Carnegie the Peacemaker

Carnegie's greatest desire was to see the world at peace. In 1907, he wrote, "I believe the next step to universal peace to be the formation of a League of Nations."[25] On November 25, 1910, his seventy-fifth birthday, Carnegie announced the creation of the Carnegie Endowment for International Peace with a fund of $10 million. Its purpose, he said, was "to hasten the abolition of war."[26] He provided money for the building of the Temple of Peace at The Hague in Holland to pursue that goal. In his spare time, he wrote numerous articles and pamphlets with titles like "Peace versus War" and "The Path of Peace Upon the Seas."

Despite Carnegie's efforts, World War I broke out in Europe in 1914 when Germany invaded Belgium and France. It was a great shock to one who loved peace as much as Carnegie. As the war raged, Carnegie felt his spirit weaken. In the early months of 1915, he suffered a bout of pneumonia. As the bright days of spring arrived, he sat sadly in his New York City garden, wrapped in blankets, unwarmed by the sun. He could not travel to Scotland during

the war. Instead, he tried to find summer comfort at Pointe d'Acadie, Bar Harbor, Maine, in 1915. For the summer of 1916, the Carnegies bought a large stone mansion called Shadowbrook near Lenox, Massachusetts.

By February 1917, Carnegie realized the United States must enter the war and help defeat Germany. After Congress declared war in April 1917, Carnegie sent a telegram to President Woodrow Wilson, saying, "You have triumphed at last. God bless you. You will give the world peace and rank the greatest hero of all."[27]

In the summer of 1917, Louise Carnegie wrote a letter from Shadowbrook: "Andrew is a new man since coming here. We take a motor drive every day and we are so delighted with the beautiful country."[28] But in truth, Carnegie missed Skibo, and he was brokenhearted waiting for the war to end.

The surrender of Germany in November 1918 raised his hopes, and the marriage of his daughter, Margaret, in April 1919 brought him joy. But on August 9, eighty-three-year-old Andrew Carnegie fell stricken once again with pneumonia. He died on August 11, 1919. Mourners carried his casket to Sleepy Hollow Cemetery in North Tarrytown, New York, for burial.

At his death, many Americans guessed Carnegie had left behind a fortune of hundreds of millions of dollars. In his will, however, his fortune was revealed

Andrew Carnegie is still remembered not only for his extraordinary success as a businessman, but for the many contributions he made through his financial gifts.

to be $23 million. He had given away 90 percent of his money in his lifetime—$324,657,399. He had not died in disgrace. He had fulfilled the duty he had given himself. At the time, Carnegie's gifts were the greatest ever distributed by one person. In old age, Carnegie himself had looked back on his career and could hardly believe it. When told how much he had given away, he exclaimed, "Where did I ever get all that money?"[29]

Truly, Andrew Carnegie had been a one-of-a-kind steelmaker and philanthropist. At Carnegie's death, former Secretary of State Elihu Root honestly declared,

> He belonged to that great race of nation-builders who have made the development of America the wonder of the world. . . . He was the kindliest man I ever knew. Wealth had brought to him no hardening of the heart, nor made him forget the dreams of his youth.[30]

Andrew Carnegie, the poor immigrant boy from Scotland, left the United States and the world a lasting legacy. His steel built railroads, bridges, skyscrapers, and ships. His gifts aided colleges, scientific projects, and social institutions. Perhaps most important of all, his many libraries have provided knowledge and entertainment for millions of people and will continue to do so far into the future.

CHRONOLOGY

1835—Born on November 25, in Dunfermline, Scotland, the son of William and Margaret Carnegie.

1843—Begins attending school; Brother, Thomas, born.

1848—Leaves Scotland with his family and settles in Allegheny, Pennsylvania; Works in a cotton mill and a bobbin factory.

1850—Begins work as a telegraph messenger in Pittsburgh.

1851—Becomes a telegraph operator.

1853—Becomes assistant to Pennsylvania Railroad Superintendent Thomas A. Scott.

1855—Father, William Carnegie, dies.

1858—Becomes partner in the Woodruff Sleeping-Car Company.

1859—Receives promotion to Western Division superintendent of the Pennsylvania Railroad.

1861—Helps organize Union military railroad and telegraph service in Washington, D.C., at the start of the Civil War; Becomes a partner in the Columbia Oil Company.

1862—Returns to Scotland for a visit.

1865—Quits the Pennsylvania Railroad and becomes a full-time private investor; Organizes the Union Iron Mills in Pittsburgh; Tours Europe with two friends.

1869—Joins forces with George Pullman to form the Pullman Palace Car Company.

1874—His Keystone Bridge Company finishes work on the St. Louis Bridge across the Mississippi River.

1875—Carnegie, McCandless & Company begins manufacturing steel rails at its Edgar Thomson Steel Works near Pittsburgh.

1878—Takes trip around the world.

1881—Merges all of his companies into Carnegie Brothers & Co.; Buys an interest in the Henry C. Frick Coke Company; Takes coaching tour of Great Britain.

1886—Mother, Margaret, and brother, Tom, die.

1887—Marries Louise Whitfield on April 22.

1889—Names Henry Clay Frick chief executive officer of his steel company.

1892—Carnegie Brothers & Co. becomes the Carnegie Steel Company; A strike at the Homestead mill ends in bloodshed.

1897—Daughter, Margaret, is born.

1900—Carnegie Steel earns an annual profit of $40 million.

1901—Sells out steel interests; Devotes himself to giving away his fortune to worthy causes; Founds the Carnegie Relief Fund, a pension fund for retired Carnegie steelworkers.

1904—Establishes the Hero Fund and the Carnegie Institution.

1911—Establishes the Carnegie Corporation with $125 million.

1919—Daughter, Margaret, marries; He dies on August 11 and is buried in North Tarrytown, New York.

CHAPTER NOTES

Chapter 1. "The Richest Man in the World"

1. Herbert N. Casson, *The Romance of Steel* (Freeport, N.Y.: A. S. Barnes & Company, 1907), p. 143.
2. Robert L. Heilbroner, "Epitaph for the Steel Master," *American Heritage*, August 1960, p. 109.
3. Harold C. Livesay, *Andrew Carnegie and the Rise of Big Business* (Boston: Little, Brown and Company, 1975), p. 185.
4. Casson, p. 186.
5. Ibid., p. 185.
6. Heilbroner, p. 110.
7. Livesay, p. 188.
8. Heilbroner, p. 4.
9. George Swetnam, *Andrew Carnegie* (Boston: Twayne Publishers, 1980), p. 48.
10. "Hall of Fame of Philanthropy," *Time*, September 1, 1997, p. 54.

Chapter 2. The Scottish Weaver's Son

1. Andrew Carnegie, *Autobiography* (Boston: Houghton Mifflin Company, 1920), p. 2.
2. Ibid., p. 13.
3. Joseph Frazier Wall, *Andrew Carnegie* (New York: Oxford University Press, 1970), p. 46.
4. Carnegie, p. 14.
5. Ibid., p. 23.
6. Harold C. Livesay, *Andrew Carnegie and the Rise of Big Business* (Boston: Little, Brown and Company, 1975), p. 7.
7. Carnegie, p. 11.
8. Wall, p. 58.
9. Carnegie, p. 13.
10. Wall, p. 65.
11. Ibid., p. 67.
12. Carnegie, p. 23–24.
13. Ibid., p. 13.
14. Wall, p. 72.

Chapter 3. Rise of an Immigrant Boy

1. Harold C. Livesay, *Andrew Carnegie and the Rise of Big Business* (Boston: Little, Brown and Company, 1975), p. 16.

2. Andrew Carnegie, *Autobiography* (Boston: Houghton Mifflin Company, 1920), pp. 31–32.

3. Ibid., p. 33.

4. Joseph Frazier Wall, *Andrew Carnegie* (New York: Oxford University Press, 1970), p. 88.

5. Livesay, p. 17.

6. John S. Bowman, *Andrew Carnegie* (Englewood Cliffs, N.J.: Silver Burdett Press, 1989), p. 25.

7. Carnegie, p. 35.

8. George Swetnam, *Andrew Carnegie* (Boston: Twayne Publishers, 1980), p. 18.

9. Carnegie, pp. 37–38.

10. Ibid.

11. Ibid., p. 41.

12. Ibid., p. 42.

13. Ibid., p. 53.

14. Bowman, p. 38.

15. Carnegie, p. 55.

16. Ibid., pp. 55–56.

17. Ibid., p. 57.

Chapter 4. Young Railroad Man

1. Joseph Frazier Wall, *Andrew Carnegie* (New York: Oxford University Press, 1970), p. 116.

2. Ibid., p. 124.

3. Andrew Carnegie, *Autobiography* (Boston: Houghton Mifflin Company, 1920), pp. 67–68.

4. George Swetnam, *Andrew Carnegie* (Boston: Twayne Publishers, 1980), p. 22.

5. Carnegie, p. 69.

6. Ibid., p. 76.

7. John S. Bowman, *Andrew Carnegie* (Englewood Cliffs, N.J.: Silver Burdett Press, 1989), p. 36.

8. Carnegie, p. 83.

9. Robert L. Heilbroner, "Epitaph for the Steel Master," *American Heritage*, August 1960, p. 9.

10. Wall, p. 129.

11. Carnegie, p. 89.

12. Bowman, p. 39.

13. David Homer Bates, *Lincoln in the Telegraph Office* (Lincoln, Nebr.: University of Nebraska Press, 1995), pp. 22–25.

14. Wall, p. 166.

15. Carnegie, p. 96.

16. Bowman, p. 44.

17. Harold C. Livesay, *Andrew Carnegie and the Rise of Big Business* (Boston: Little, Brown and Company, 1975), p. 41.

18. Wall, p. 189.

Chapter 5. Investor and Industrialist

1. Andrew Carnegie, *Autobiography* (Boston: Houghton Mifflin Company, 1920), p. 135.

2. Robert L. Heilbroner, "Epitaph for the Steel Master," *American Heritage*, August 1960, p. 9.

3. Ibid., p. 107.

4. James Howard Bridge, *The Inside History of the Carnegie Steel Company* (New York: Arno Press, 1972), p. 42.

5. Joseph Frazier Wall, *Andrew Carnegie* (New York: Oxford University Press, 1970), p. 277.

6. Ibid., p. 291.

7. Harold C. Livesay, *Andrew Carnegie and the Rise of Big Business* (Boston: Little, Brown and Company, 1975), p. 56.

8. Ibid., p. 57.

9. Carnegie, p. 170.

10. Bridge, pp. 55–56.

11. Ibid., p. 75.

12. Livesay, p. 80.

13. Wall, p. 264.

14. John S. Bowman, *Andrew Carnegie* (Englewood Cliffs, N.J.: Silver Burdett Press, 1989), p. 63.

Chapter 6. The Steel King

1. Joseph Frazier Wall, *Andrew Carnegie* (New York: Oxford University Press, 1970), p. 295.

2. Ibid., p. 320.

3. Harold C. Livesay, *Andrew Carnegie and the Rise of Big Business* (Boston: Little, Brown and Company, 1975), p. 96.

4. James Howard Bridge, *The Inside History of the Carnegie Steel Company* (New York: Arno Press, 1972), pp. 78–79.

5. Wall, p. 346.

6. Bridge, p. 81.

7. Herbert N. Casson, *The Romance of Steel* (Freeport, N.Y.: A. S. Barnes & Company, 1907), p. 30.

8. Bridge, p. 143.

9. Casson, pp. 142–143.

10. Wall, p. 346.

11. Livesay, p. 112.

12. Bridge, p. 85.

13. Casson, p. 128.

14. Livesay, p. 111.

15. Casson, p. 28.

16. Wall, p. 527.

17. Casson, p. 29.

18. Livesay, p. 101.

Chapter 7. Man of the World

1. George Swetnam, *Andrew Carnegie* (Boston: Twayne Publishers, 1980), p. 32.

2. Andrew Carnegie, *Round the World* (New York: Charles Scribner's Sons, 1884), p. 1.

3. Joseph Frazier Wall, *Andrew Carnegie* (New York: Oxford University Press, 1970), p. 374.

4. Carnegie, p. 333.

5. Swetnam, p. 100.

6. Wall, p. 402.

7. John S. Bowman, *Andrew Carnegie* (Englewood Cliffs, N.J.: Silver Burdett Press, 1989), p. 72.

8. Wall, pp. 404–405.

9. Andrew Carnegie, *An American Four-In-Hand in Britain* (New York: Charles Scribner's Sons, 1891), p. 150.

10. Ibid., p. 240.

11. Carnegie, *Round the World*, p. 1.

12. Swetnam, p. 45.

13. Bowman, p. 83.

14. Robert L. Heilbroner, "Epitaph for the Steel Master," *American Heritage*, August 1960, p. 6.

15. Harold C. Livesay, *Andrew Carnegie and the Rise of Big Business* (Boston: Little, Brown and Company, 1975), p. 128.

16. Wall, p. 832.

Chapter 8. Tragedy and Triumph

1. Joseph Frazier Wall, *Andrew Carnegie* (New York: Oxford University Press, 1970), p. 419.

2. Harold C. Livesay, *Andrew Carnegie and the Rise of Big Business* (Boston: Little, Brown and Company, 1975), p. 127.

3. Wall, p. 497.

4. Ibid., p. 536.

5. James Howard Bridge, *The Inside History of the Carnegie Steel Company* (New York: Arno Press, 1972), p. 169.

6. Livesay, p. 128.

7. John S. Bowman, *Andrew Carnegie* (Englewood Cliffs, N.J.: Silver Burdett Press, 1989), p. 89.

8. Robert L. Reynolds, "The Works Are Not Worth One Drop of Human Blood," *American Heritage*, August 1960, p. 109.

9. Bridge, p. 214.

10. Ibid., p. 217.

11. Wall, p. 559.

12. Reynolds, p. 109.

13. Livesay, p. 142.

14. Bridge, pp. 233–234.

15. Andrew Carnegie, *Autobiography* (Boston: Houghton Mifflin Company, 1920), p. 223.

16. Livesay, pp. 150–151.

17. Ibid., p. 152.

18. Ibid., p. 154.

19. Wall, p. 609.

20. Livesay, p. 170.

21. Ibid., p. 169.

22. Bridge, p. 295.

23. Wall, pp. 759–760.

24. Heilbroner, p. 110.

Chapter 9. The Great Philanthropist

1. Herbert N. Casson, *The Romance of Steel* (Freeport, N.Y.: A. S. Barnes & Company, 1907), p. 203.

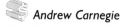

Andrew Carnegie

2. Joseph Frazier Wall, *Andrew Carnegie* (New York: Oxford University Press, 1970), p. 790.

3. Ibid., p. 857.

4. Ibid., p. 825.

5. Ibid., p. 831.

6. Ibid., pp. 836–837.

7. Ibid., pp. 818–819.

8. Ibid., pp. 826–827.

9. Andrew Carnegie, *Autobiography* (Boston: Houghton Mifflin Company, 1920), p. 45.

10. Wall, p. 819.

11. Ibid., pp. 828–829.

12. Ibid., p. 826.

13. Robert L. Heilbroner, "Epitaph for the Steel Master," *American Heritage*, August 1960, p. 111.

14. Wall, pp. 893–894.

15. Ibid., p. 830.

16. Carnegie, p. 250.

17. Wall, p. 862.

18. Ibid., pp. 864–866.

19. Ibid., p. 868.

20. Ibid., p. 796.

21. Ibid., pp. 882–883.

22. Ibid., p. 942.

23. John S. Bowman, *Andrew Carnegie* (Englewood Cliffs, N.J.: Silver Burdett Press, 1989), p. 85.

24. Wall, p. 847.

25. Ibid., p. 921.

26. Ibid., p. 898.

27. Ibid., p. 1034.

28. Ibid.

29. Heilbroner, p. 4.

30. Carnegie, p. 265.

GLOSSARY

alloy—A mixture of two or more basic metals.

anarchist—A person dedicated to destroying government and order.

batten—On a loom, the long strip of wood that holds the woven threads in place.

billet—A bar of metal.

bond—A certificate promising interest on a loan.

botany—The study of plant life.

capital—Accumulated possessions or wealth.

dividends—Company profits distributed from time to time to shareholders of stock.

fireman—A stoker who feeds an engine with fuel.

gauntlet—A double row of people, facing each other and armed with weapons.

geophysics—The study of the earth's energy and movements, including volcanoes, earthquakes, and oceans.

ingot—A mass of metal cast into a convenient shape for storage or transportation.

linen—A cloth woven from the stringy fiber of the flax plant.

loom—A frame or machine used for weaving threads or yarns into cloth.

molten—Made liquid by heat.

nutrition—The process of good health through the proper use of food.

patent—A document securing to an inventor the exclusive right to make, use, or sell his or her invention.

philanthropy—Goodwill toward fellow humans, especially by kind acts or gifts.

pneumonia—A disease in which the lungs become inflamed and filled with liquid.

rabies—A viral disease of the nervous system transmitted by the bite of a rabid animal.

revenue—The total income produced by an individual or company.

sociology—The study of society and the behavior of humans in organized groups.

textile—Cloth.

treadle—A device to drive a machine, operated by the pressure of the foot.

typhoid—A disease marked by high fever, usually caused by the bites of body lice or passed from human to human.

woof—A woven thread or yarn.

FURTHER READING

Books

Bates, David Homer. *Lincoln in the Telegraph Office*. Lincoln, Nebr.: University of Nebraska Press, 1995.

Bowman, John S. *Andrew Carnegie*. Englewood Cliffs, N.J.: Silver Burdett Press, 1989.

Carnegie, Andrew. *Autobiography*. Boston: Houghton Mifflin Company, 1920.

Kent, Zachary. *The Story of the Battle of Bull Run*. Chicago: Children's Press, 1986.

McCormick, Anita Louise. *The Industrial Revolution in American History*. Springfield, N.J.: Enslow Publishers, Inc., 1998.

Shippen, Katherine. *Andrew Carnegie and the Age of Steel*. New York: Random House, 1958.

Simon, Charlie May. *The Andrew Carnegie Story*. New York: E. P. Dutton & Co., 1965.

Internet Sites

Carnegie Library of Pittsburgh. October 1994. <http://www.clpgh.org/exhibit/carnegie.html> (July 2, 1998).

Public Broadcasting Service. "The Richest Man in the World: Andrew Carnegie." *The American Experience*. 1998. <http://www.pbs.org/wgbh/pages/amex/carnegie/milltour> (July 2, 1998).

INDEX